Political Economy in the Twentieth Century

Edited by

Maxine Berg

University of Warwick

Philip Allan

New York London Toronto Sydney Tokyo Singapore

First published 1990 by
Philip Allan
66 Wood Lane End, Hemel Hempstead
Hertfordshire, HP2 4RG
A division of
Simon & Schuster International Group

Printed and bound in Great Britain by
Billings and Sons Ltd, Worcester

British Library Cataloguing in Publication Data

Political economy in the twentieth century
1. Economics. Theories, 1900-1986
I. Berg, Maxine
330.1

ISBN 0 86003-803-3
ISBN 0-86003-903-X PbK

1 2 3 4 5 94 93 92 91 90

POLITICAL ECONOMY IN THE TWENTIETH CENTURY

Contents

List of Contributors

Maxine Berg is Senior Lecturer in Economic History at the University of Warwick.

Amartya Sen is Professor of Economics at Harvard University.

G.C. Harcourt is University Lecturer in Economics and Politics at Cambridge University, Fellow and President of Jesus College, Cambridge University.

Malcolm Sawyer is Professor of Economics at the University of York.

Joseph Steindl is Emeritus Professor at the Osterreichisches Institut für Wirtschaftsforschung, Vienna.

Tom Bottomore is Emeritus Professor of Sociology at the University of Sussex.

Michael Lebowitz is Professor of Economics at Simon Fraser University, Canada.

1

Historical Introduction

MAXINE BERG

This book is based on a series of lectures given at Warwick University in 1986. The lectures were designed to gather together some leading economists and historians to discuss the work of a select number of major intellectuals of twentieth-century political economy. These were not to be the figures who dominated the established neoclassical or even Keynesian traditions of economics. They stood, rather, outside the mainstream, acting as critics of the Western capitalist order and of the theory which seeks to explain it.

The group selected here is broadly based: Piero Sraffa, Joan Robinson, Maurice Dobb, Michal Kalecki, Josef Steindl, Joseph Schumpeter and Paul Sweezy. These economists were by no means all Marxists or even left-wing critics: *vide* Joseph Schumpeter. Their work was, nevertheless, influenced by Marx, however much some of them may have disagreed with him. More generally, a number of these economists revived and continued the tradition of classical and Marxist economics in a twentieth-century context. This was a tradition broader in scope than the established approaches, much more self-conscious about its assumptions about society and the individual and prepared to tackle the fundamental issues of accumulation and the distribution of the surplus.

The work of the chosen group has itself been profoundly influential in establishing a critical tradition in economics, a tradition based both on alternative theory and on the significance of historical understanding. Major intellectuals though they were, all these figures always remained on the outside of their discipline.

Some imported the perspectives of the European intelligentsia; others reacted against a cultural establishment or brought to bear longer traditions of intellectual dissent. They formed the critical conscience, the dissident voice of an economic theory increasingly without historical framework, political relevance or a dynamic perspective on the future of capitalism.

This collection is, however, more than a study of leading intellectuals. It is also a study of the principal problems and theoretical inheritance which linked together theorists of otherwise disparate social and political contexts. These theorists were bound together by their interest in two key issues arising out of Marxist economic theory: the processes of capitalist accumulation and development on the one hand, and the distribution of the surplus and the sources of profit on the other. A number of these economists adopted or at least aspired to provide an overtly historical framework for their theory; hence their great interest in the phases of capitalist development. The common thread through much of their work lies in historical theories of capitalist cycles and the tendencies within capitalist economies for phases of growth to alternate with decline and even long-term stagnation. This focus was combined in most with a belief in the classical and Marxist view of the significance of the distribution of the surplus.

Though some of the individuals included here were of very different political persuasions, their intellectual backgrounds and connections were similar. There are many other outstanding dissident economists from these generations: Veblen and Galbraith offered their own idiosyncratic critiques; Sweezy's collaborators Paul Baran and Harry Magdoff made their own substantial contribution, while Kalecki's colleague, Oskar Lange, offered an influential market socialism. And Nicholas Kaldor was as significant as Joan Robinson in developing the post-Keynesian school. These economists are not included in this study, which purposely dwells on only a small number of leading figures and seeks to establish a few central connections between them, connections which have established the framework for the critique of economic theory in this century.

Keynes is not included in this discussion of political economy: this may need a word of explanation. Keynes's work had a great influence on most of the critics included in this collection and especially on Robinson, Kalecki, Steindl and Sweezy. Keynes is not included here partly because he is already the subject of a great many historical works and partly because his work has, at least since the war, been considered to lie at the centre of establishment traditions of economics. Although an effective critic of unregulated capitalism, Keynes did not go so far as to question the basic tenets of the capitalist system itself. His theory, while 'revolutionary' *within* economic theory, constituting a new intellectual paradigm, did not challenge the *framework* of that theory. Keynes was not a rebel against the Cambridge tradition established by Marshall and developed by Pigou and D. H. Robertson. Though he came to have important theoretical disagreements with this other Cambridge school, his work was initially based on the same foundations. In keeping with this tradition, his work was much more directly opposed to the Austrian–LSE school of market-clearing simultaneity.[1]

Keynes accepted the traditional neoclassical theory of value and the marginal productivity theory of distribution. His model in the *General Theory* usually assumed perfect competition and a closed economy.[2] Joan Robinson later described the *General Theory* as 'narrow'. There was 'little on international trade', and though the influence of the flow of investment on employment was central, there was 'little on accumulation as a historical process'.[3] Finally, one of the key theoretical divides between Keynes and most of his critics was his lack of interest in the classical question of the distribution of income between different classes of the community: he did not raise questions about the formation of the overall rate of profit.[4] One result of this lack of interest in class distribution was his use of concepts such as the 'propensity to consume', denounced by Schumpeter as 'pseudo psychology'.[5] Another result of Keynes's marriage of revolutionary questioning of the content and assumptions of economic theory with much of the apparatus and conventions of neoclassicism was the failure of mainstream economics to challenge the basic precepts of microeconomics. Keynesian ideas became a part of macroeconomics, while microeconomic theory returned to the analysis of general equilibrium.[6] Above all, Keynesian theory became accepted as a new orthodoxy itself. Though Keynes's own intentions may well have differed from what was later read into his theory, it was certainly the case that in the hand of his successors, it joined the establishment: in its simplified versions it was grafted on to the

Walrasian general equilibrium tradition.

Keynes was a man of intellectual vision, a broader thinker than any other mainstream economist of his day. He was always greatly concerned with policy issues and the active management of the economy. But he was never a socialist and was relatively ignorant of Marx and Marxian traditions. He treated *Capital* as 'an obsolete economics textbook' which was 'not only scientifically erroneous but without interest or application for the modern world'. Indeed, Marx was placed in company with Major Douglas, the right-wing exponent of theories of social credit.[7] But although Keynes had little direct impact on the Left of the Labour Party before the war, some of his key followers were more influential. James Meade, as a member of the New Fabians, expressed complete faith in the Keynesian system and developed theoretical and practical applications of Keynesian economics. One of those whom Meade in turn influenced was Douglas Jay, author of the *Socialist Case* (1937), which played an important part in 'adapting Keynesian analysis to socialist goals for the Labour Party'.[8] This legacy of Keynes's was also to inspire the progressive Keynesian social democracy that was to dominate Labour Party thinking in the post-war period and the 1960s. Keynes revolutionised mainstream economic theory but he did not stand outside that mainstream either as a critic of society or of capitalism as a system.

Yet in spite of this it is clear that Keynes exerted a fundamental intellectual impact on many of those included in the volume. Robinson, Kalecki, Steindl and Sweezy perhaps owed more to him than to any other single intellectual influence. Placing Keynes within this selected group of political economists is difficult: he was not one of them and yet he was directly influential. Most of the essays in the volume discuss his particular influence in some depth, so that though he is not the subject of a separate chapter, his presence is never absent.

I will now proceed to a brief introduction to the lives and work of the theorists under consideration in the book.

I

Piero Sraffa, Joan Robinson and Maurice Dobb are all closely related figures who drew on Marxian and Keynesian argument within the context of Cambridge economics. Sraffa was born in

Turin in 1898, the son of a well-known lawyer and professor of commercial law. He was a committed socialist from his youth and a friend of Gramsci's. Sraffa settled in England in 1927, but remained deeply influenced by Gramsci and at his suggestion turned away from his early preoccupation with the problems of money and banking to the issues raised by the classical theory of value.

The other major influence on Sraffa's work was Ricardo. Sraffa developed the main ideas of his neo-Ricardian theory of value before he came to England but did not take them up again in any depth until the 1950s. He published two influential papers in the 1920s: the first, in 1925, aimed to show the logical incoherence of Marshall's method; the other, published in 1926, 'The laws of returns under competitive conditions', included a section about monopoly which helped to encourage work on imperfect competition. These papers impressed the leading Cambridge economists — Pigou, Robertson and Keynes — and assured Sraffa of a place in Cambridge. Sraffa's life's work was subsequently taken up with an exhaustive and meticulous edition of Ricardo's works. The introduction to the first volume, *The Principles*, offers the closest definitive exposition and analysis of the Ricardian theory of exchange value.

But the book which set out his alternative theory of value and distribution, *Production of Commodities by Means of Commodities*, was not published until 1960. Sraffa's purpose was to give a 'new formulation of the classical view of the circular nature of the production process, (going back to the Physiocrats)'.[9] The book was to provide the basis for a critique of marginalist theories of wages, profits, rents and prices. It demonstrated the relations between wages, profits, prices and conditions of production, established the dependence of prices, of the 'value of capital' and of the choice of technique on income distribution.[10]

Sraffa accepted the Marxian framework overall and saw his task as to fill in some unfinished parts of Marx's work.[11] But his work did more than undermine the analytical foundations of neoclassical economics. Some of Sraffa's followers, notably Garegnani, Pasinetti, Bharadwaj and Eatwell continued to do this, but others, such as Steedman, used his analysis to challenge the place of Marx's labour theory of value in the determination of the rate of profit.[12]

Joan Robinson came from an academic family with a long tradition of intellectual dissent. Her early work in economics was based on Marshallian principles. Though these principles structured her first major work, *The Economics of Imperfect Competition* (1933), she was critical of the central focus of economic theory on theories of perfect competition. The book was 'inspired by the "pregnant suggestion" in Sraffa's 1926 *Economic Journal* article concerning the generality of monopoly rather than competition as the way forward in the theory of value'.[13] Joan Robinson was part of the Cambridge 'circus', a small discussion group which included Austin Robinson, Sraffa, Kahn and Meade, who argued out the questions raised first by Keynes's *Treatise on Money* and then *The General Theory*, and extended his analysis by working to develop a long-period theory of effective demand and to develop the international aspects of Keynesian theory.[14]

Reading Marx and the influence of Michal Kalecki were the major factors pushing Joan Robinson towards a much more critical view of economic theory. It was the war which pushed her decisively to the left. But Sraffa remained the dominant intellectual force in her life. Her views of Marxian economics were set out in the *Essay on Marxian Economics* (1942) and in her introduction to Rosa Luxemburg's *Accumulation of Capital* (1951) and in many later articles.[15] Marx's reproduction schemes were the starting point for Rosa Luxemburg's and then Kalecki's theories of effective demand, the trade cycle and capitalist crisis; Joan Robinson, too, used them as the starting point for her work on capital and growth. Under these influences, as well as Sraffa's, she developed the dynamic analysis of her *magnum opus*, *The Accumulation of Capital* (1956). In later life she turned increasingly to a methodological critique of neoclassical economic theory.

Maurice Dobb's critical perspectives do not find their source in family traditions of academic influence. Coming from a family of small businessmen, he became involved in socialist and labour politics before attending university. He had much more established historical interests than either Sraffa or Robinson and though he studied economics at Cambridge, economic history was a subject which continued to attract him. His early reading was on English socialism — the guild socialists and the Webbs — and a few Marxist classics: *Capital* and Lenin's *State and Revolution*, along with a few continental social and historical critics, Labriola, Croce and Sorel. He was one of the first English economists to explicitly apply Marx's theory of surplus value and exploitation,[16] and he became a member of the Communist Party soon after it was founded.[17] Dobb's socialism was much more political than either Sraffa's or Robinson's: he was politically active from the time he left school and wrote prolifically for workers' education and public debate. He became one of the most outstanding political economists of the century. It was he who established Marxian economics on a broad front in the UK, working over a wide range of fields: Marxist economic theory, welfare and planning, the Soviet economy, development economics, the history of economic thought. His work also included a notable contribution to the debate on the transition from feudalism to capitalism, *Studies in the Development of Capitalism* (Routledge 1946).

Dobb's book, *Political Economy and Capitalism* (1937), was his major original contribution to Marxist economic theory. In it he attempted to explain and defend the Marxian approach in a way that would be comprehensible to those trained in the Marshallian tradition.[18] It was at this stage that he developed his distinctive, descriptive approach to the labour theory of value. Dobb saw value theory as a means of depicting productive activities in terms of human involvement. He set out this approach in his paper, 'The requirements of a theory of value'.[19] In this paper Dobb set out what a value theory does, why it is interesting, why it is important and what its role is. The theory of value in Dobb's analysis is primarily a way of describing what is happening with production structure. He saw the labour theory of value as a way of emphasising the role of those who are involved in 'personal participation' in the process of production, as opposed to those who have no such personal involvement. He continued this approach, pointing out the descriptive poverty of the marginal productivity theory of distribution. Such a theory made an illicit link between ownership and production, imputing to the owner the productivity of the things he 'owned'. His descriptive labour theory, while explicitly rejecting utility theory, nevertheless incorporated the significance of wants and needs.[20]

Dobb was later distinctive among English Marxist economists for standing aloof from the fracas of the transformation problem. But in his 1973 volume, *Theories of Value and Distribution since Adam Smith*,[21] he did appear to endorse the Sraffian approach. His reasons for this, as Amartya Sen argues, were to be found in feelings of solidarity with others who challenged orthodox economics. Dobb expressed impatience with those who were divided over this critique of orthodox economics. In his last journal article, published just before his death, he responded to the Cambridge critique and the neo-Ricardians:

> when such an ideological contest is being joined I would suggest that Marxists have more to gain by stressing what they have *in common* with their allies, in the shape of fellow critics of prevailing bourgeois orthodoxy, who would not perhaps go all the way with them in positive statements of what they believe; and that it is weakening and divisive, (and in this sense sectarian), to focus attention on differences between Marxists, near Marxists and others... The sectarian critics have, in my view, much underestimated the extent to which rehabilitating Ricardo, for the great majority of people schooled in orthodox teaching... is ipso facto an introduction to the study of Marx.[22]

Dobb, like Robinson, was later influenced by Kalecki and came to rewrite the chapter on economic crises in his *Political Economy and Capitalism*. Dobb was also well known for his work on growth and development, socialist planning and his histories of the Russian and Soviet economies.

His work was much more historical in its approach, methods and interests than Sraffa's and Robinson's. His interpretation of Marx's theory of value gave a historian's emphasis to descriptive richness. His concern with detail, then with selection, then with producing from both a story or explanation, is a historical methodology. But this methodology was also, as Dobb argued, necessary to economic theory. He looked at theories of crisis from an historian's perspective, emphasising the observed phenomena of slumps and depressions; and he was always interested in the long-run features of capitalist development.[23] His work in the divergent areas of economic theory, applied economics and economic history was thus closely related.

But it was the *Studies in the Development of Capitalism* (1946) which really laid out the lines of Dobb's historical approach to the analysis of capitalist development, and it was this book which introduced Marxist approaches and methods to a broad audience. The book was not just a Marxist history; it was an attempt to reorientate the line of Marxist research away from static problems, such as disputes over the theory of value, to a dynamic analysis of capitalism.[24] Dobb made use of history to explore his view that the capitalist class was born out of the ranks of production itself. He elaborated Marx's suggestion of 'the really revolutionary way' to capitalist development, arguing in the *Studies* that the decisive steps to capitalist social production relations are taken by the artisans and former petty producers who hire wage labour and bring in new techniques. Capitalists, in other words, emerged from the ranks of artisans and yeomen, and 'made the bourgeois revolution against the landlords and merchants'.[25] Paul Sweezy's review of *Studies* started the classic debate on the transition from feudalism to capitalism.

Both Joan Robinson and Maurice Dobb were influenced at an early stage of their work by the Polish economist Michal Kalecki. Kalecki and his Austrian follower, Josef Steindl, developed Marxist-based analyses of the dynamic of capitalist development and connected these to the role of monopoly structures.

Michal Kalecki's work in economics was always outside the mainstream tradition. His first reading in economics was Rosa Luxemburg, Tugan-Baranovski and Marx. A training in engineering and early practical work on specific industry studies at the Research Institute of Business Cycles and Prices in Warsaw made a major contribution to his distinctive approach.

Kalecki is generally compared to Keynes; he is known for developing a theory similar to Keynes's but failing to receive due professional recognition for his achievement. But the comparison does not bear close scrutiny. Kalecki's background, priorities and the framework for his theory were explicitly socialist. From the early 1930s in Poland he identified with the intellectual wing of the socialist movement and contributed articles on economic and political themes to *Przeqlad Socjalistczny*. Kalecki's inspiration came not so much from reading Marxist texts as from experiencing economic depression and his 'revulsion at the brutalities of capitalist society and a wish for a better system'.[26] Kalecki's socialism marked him off from Keynes: he had no interest in preserving the free enterprise system and advocated state intervention on the basis of his socialist beliefs.[27]

Like Dobb, Kalecki also wrote widely in political economy but from a much more policy-based position. Kalecki's macro-economics, based on assumptions of imperfect competition, was and is widely influential; but equally significant were his contributions to work on cyclical fluctuations, employment, the war economy, socialist planning and development studies. Policy work provided the stimulation, focus and empirical basis of his work. In 1935 he left the Business Cycles and Prices Research Institute in Warsaw where he had analysed particular commodity markets, and then went first to Sweden, then to the LSE and Cambridge. While he was at Cambridge he took an active part in Sraffa's seminar on costs and prices in industry and also worked on the Cambridge research scheme of the National Institute of Economic and Social Research into prime costs, proceeds and output.[28] In 1940 he came to the Oxford Institute of Statistics where he was in charge of a programme on war finance, writing regular analyses of the financial situation. From Oxford he went to the UN Secretariat where he produced his famous *World Economic Reports* until 1955 when McCarthyism and political pressures on his work prompted his return to Poland. In Poland he was for a time a member of the Central School of Planning and Statistics, Vice-Chairman of the Economic Council and an important member of the Planning Commission.[29]

Kalecki's first major theoretical work, *Outline of a Theory of the Business Cycle*, published in Polish in 1933, was the work which contained a model similar to Keynes's to explain fluctuations in the level of effective demand and employment in capitalist countries. But Kalecki's model was based on assumptions of oligopoly and class distribution rather than perfect competition and psychological factors. In Kalecki's model, profits were related to total national income by a linear relation determined by the firm's mark up; this reflected market power which in turn determined distribution. In contrast to the 'psychologism' of Keynes's 'propensity to consume', Kalecki divided the 'man' in his theory of effective demand into workers and capitalists. Finally, he set out the identity between savings and investment in such a way as to make the time lag between investment decisions and actual investment explicit, so that investment was predetermined by decisions made in the past.[30]

It was not just Kalecki's socialism and his ideas which placed him outside the mainstream. His approach was unconventional. While he liked mathematical precision and expressed his ideas in neat formulae, he also used history, politics and institutions. Joan Robinson has, in fact, argued that in the USA Keynes's theory was absorbed into the neoclassical synthesis; but Kalecki's work was indigestible and therefore ignored.[31] But some of Kalecki's best-known essays were those which explored his views of politics and economic policy. His famous 'Political aspects of full employment', (1943) predicted the shift in political objectives away from full employment. And *The Last Phase in the Transformation of Capitalism* (Monthly Review Press 1972) contained his essays on armaments and militarisation, Fascism and political aspects of the business cycle.

Kalecki worked at the Institute of Economics and Statistics in Oxford with a group of refugees which included Burchardt, Mandelbaum, Schumacher, Steindl, Balogh and Frankel. He influenced most of his colleagues, but in Josef Steindl particularly he found the disciple who carried on his work in a major study of cyclical fluctuation and stagnation.

Josef Steindl's early training in economics was in a European tradition: that of the Austrian economists, especially Böhm-Bawerk. But an early concern with unemployment brought him under the influence of Keynes. As an *émigré*, after the German occupation, he worked with Kalecki at the Oxford Institute of Economics and Statistics. Though not directly influenced by Marxist economic theory, Steindl was heavily influenced by Marx's historical perspective and by Kalecki's strongly held socialist convictions. At Kalecki's suggestion he started his project of explaining the 'crisis of capitalism' by writing on maturity and stagnation in the USA. He sought to explain the gradual slowing down of the growth rate of accumulation from the nineteenth century to the depression of the 1930s, relating this to long-term trends of accumulation and oligopolistic organisation. Steindl's book, *Maturity and Stagnation in American Capitalism* (1952),[32] appeared at a time when there was little interest in stagnation. But from the 1970s onwards interest in Steindl's work grew; it inspired Baran and Sweezy's work on monopoly capital and a tradition of work based on the market and industrial structure.

Steindl's book made the point that the theoretical mechanism of distribution in a competitive economy no longer works when an economy with many producers is replaced by oligopoly. When growth rates fall, oligopolistic producers behave differently from producers in a competitive economy: oligopolistic producers are prepared to accept lower long-term rates of utilisation rather than engage in cut-throat competition. The weight of economic adjustment to slower growth is thus thrown on to utilisation, with adverse effects on investment and further growth. Steindl defined the state of maturity as one in which the economy and its profit function are adjusted to the high growth rates of earlier stages of capitalist development, at a time when those growth rates no longer obtain.

Steindl located the reason for the decline in growth rates in the structural features of oligopoly. He assumed that the transition to oligopoly would be accompanied by greater profit margins or mark ups and thus an upward shift in the profit function. The result would not be an increase in profits for the economy as a whole since these are determined by investment. But the attempt by oligopolists to increase profits would lower utilisation and reduce incentives for investment. Lower utilisation would then create fears of generating excess capacity, so that even if the firm's total profits had not declined, investment in the next period would fall. The setback in the growth rate would therefore be cumulative; the general prediction of stagnation for the inter-war economy demonstrated a significant connection between economic fluctuations and oligopolistic or monopolistic structures. But the more general theoretical significance of Steindl's theory was lost in the context of the post-war boom, for his theory manifestly failed to provide for the possibility of this upswing. He later admitted the place of innovation, in the form of a 'technological wave', and regretted his early denial of the influence of innovation on the accumulation of capital.[33]

Steindl has written widely in the 1970s and 1980s on economic policy and aspects of stagnation theory. The economic climate has recently been much more conducive to a revival of interest in the theses of *Maturity and Stagnation*. He has also commented on trends in economic theory, and especially radical economics, in a way which places his work in a specific context. He has deplored the rise of separatist Marxist economics which has left the mainstream of economic theory intact. He blames this on the priority many Marxists have given to theoretical exegesis above the problems of current economic policy. He has had little interest in the theory of value, finding the dynamic aspects of Marx's theories more useful to his aim of explaining the development of capitalism. Like Dobb, he has taken an historical approach to explaining this process, using the tools of economic analysis.

The work of Steindl and Kalecki focused on the dynamic problems of economic cycles, capitalist accumulation and stagnation. The work of Joseph Schumpeter, written from a quite different political viewpoint, has also focused on these key problems.

At first glance Joseph Schumpeter sits oddly with this group of left-wing and dissident political economists. He accepted the conventional economics of his day and admired the circular flow analysis of general equilibrium. Although he was politically distant from the Left he maintained a close personal relationship with Sweezy. Schumpeter is one of the outstanding political economists of the period for the historical framework and vision of his work, for his analysis of the processes of capitalist accumulation and for the influence his work has had on political economy.

Schumpeter's aristocratic Austro–Hungarian background included close contact with the Austrian school of economics. He claimed that the ideas in his *Theory of Economic Development* went back to 1907 and owed much to his great teacher Böhm-Bawerk. It was with this book that he began his work on theories of interest and the business cycle, relating these to profits, money and credit. He argues that these phenomena were but 'incidents of a distinct process', in contrast to the 'theory of equilibrium which has been and still is at the centre of the traditional theory'.[34] But Schumpeter also came into early contact with the work of the Austro–Marxists, Otto Bauer, Karl Renner and Rudolf Hilferding. His interest in imperialism was first stimulated by what he called neo-Marxist theory; he attempted to offer a critique and alternative theory to that of Bauer and Hilferding.[35] Schumpeter also took a great deal from Hilferding's *Finance Capital*, especially the concept of 'organised capitalism'.

Schumpeter's analysis of capitalism as a system, his 'dynamics of capitalist accumulation', and the significance he gave to cyclical fluctuations and big business place his work firmly within the same framework as that of most of the economists discussed here. He took the view that the capitalist system was geared to incessant economic change and that its very nature implied recurrent industrial revolutions. Like Marx, he saw capitalism as a transitory phenomenon; he analysed its instabilities and predicted its decline.[36]

The subtitle Schumpeter gave to his study, *Business Cycles*, was

A Theoretical, Historical and Statistical Analysis of the Capitalist Process. But his business cycles had no Marxian tendency to worsen, for Schumpeter's entrepreneurs checked each other by competition. Unlike Keynes and Hansen, who predicted the possibility of excessive unemployment from *laissez-faire* capitalism, and unlike Steindl and Kalecki who predicted stagnation from the oligopolistic tendencies of capitalism, Schumpeter took the view that capitalism would be destroyed by its own economic success. He defined capitalism in terms of the entrepreneurial function, a function which was whittled away in the course of capitalist development. He believed in a psychology of a non-hedonistic character behind entrepreneurship and in the significance of pecuniary success as the motor of economic development. But arguing self-consciously after Marx, he predicted the emergence of a big business sector which would expropriate small and medium-sized firms and weaken the political position of the industrial bourgeoisie so that its sense of property and will to fight would disappear.

Schumpeter described big business as the 'midway house on the road to socialism'. 'The capitalist process itself produces, as effectively as it produces motorcars or refrigerators, a distribution of political power, an attitude of public mind, and an orientation of the political sector that are at variance with its own law of life.'[37] In his widely influential work, *Capitalism, Socialism and Democracy*, Schumpeter set out the wider sociological, political and cultural developments which were acting to destroy the institutional framework of capitalism. Though his political affinities were with the capitalist ethic, Schumpeter, no less than any of the Marxist critics, predicted that capitalism would break down because of the rise of 'trustified capitalism', big business and the economic role of the state; ultimately there would be a transition to socialism, which he conceived to be a system where the economic affairs of society belonged to the public, not to the private, sphere.[38]

Schumpeter did not create his own school of economics. Indeed, it was said of his teaching methods that he never imposed his own views and indeed rarely even mentioned his own writings on the subjects he taught. He had a high regard for his students and created a context of intellectual debate and excitement in which they could flourish. He believed the third decade of life to be the period of genuine creativity — 'that period of sacred fertility'.[39] But these very methods did leave disciples of his theories and of his large historical framework. One of the greatest of these was the Marxist economist Paul Sweezy.

Paul Sweezy, born into wealthy establishment circles and educated at elite private schools and Harvard, tired of the conventional economics he was schooled in. The events of the Depression turned him to the Left and he became one of America's leading Marxist economists. But Schumpeter taught Sweezy at Harvard and left his legacy clearly stamped on all of Sweezy's major work. Most of Sweezy's work was not within traditional academic institutions but founding, editing and writing for America's leading radical journal, *Monthly Review*. Sweezy founded this in 1949 but was already by then a contributor to *Science and Society*, which had been started in 1936.

Sweezy saw his task as developing a Marxist economics whose purpose was not the interpretation of texts but understanding a new phase of capitalist development, one marked by the rise of monopolies and the exploitation of the Third World. He divided Marxist approaches into traditional Marxist and neo-Marxist. He argued that traditionalists looked only to *Capital* and did not deal with monopoly capital. He followed Hilferding, Luxemburg and Lenin, then Kalecki and Steindl, in setting out the special structures of advanced capitalism and its connections with the growth of monopoly. He also argued that much of the Marxist economics of the period when *Monthly Review* was founded were Eurocentric: it saw the history of the rest of the world as repeating that of Europe. The newer Marxism which he, and especially his friend and colleague, Paul Baran, sought to develop gave central place to the role of colonies and strategies for Third World liberation movements. Paul Baran's *Political Economy of Growth* (1957) provided the cornerstone for this rethinking of world history.[40]

Baran and Sweezy started their great work, *Monopoly Capital* (1966), with a critique of Marxist economics along these lines. They argued that Marxian social science was stagnant because it continued to rest on an assumption of a competitive economy, an assumption manifestly at odds with the real world. Marx had treated monopolies not as an essential element of capitalism but as the remnants of the feudal mercantilist past and had abstracted from them. Engels had commented on the growth of monopolies in the 1880s and 1890s, but had not incorporated an analysis of them into the body of Marxian economic theory. Hilferding was the first to do this in *Finanzkapital*, but he too had seen the phenomenon as yielding merely quantitative modifications to the basic Marxian laws of capitalism, not as an altogether new element.[41] Sweezy found the first step to a real theory of monopoly capitalism in Kalecki's concept of the 'degree of monopoly'. Kalecki had demonstrated the impact of monopoly not only on the concentration of surplus value, but on the slower growth of wages. The long-run result was a bias toward over-accumulation. But it was Steindl's *Maturity and Stagnation in American Capitalism* (1952) which was the real inspiration. Sweezy wrote that this book was 'both one of the most important and most neglected works of political economy of the last half century'. Steindl had connected the American depression of the 1930s to the growth of monopoly and the resulting retarding effect of this on the centralisation of capital.[42] *Monopoly Capital* went back to the theory of the tendency to stagnation in capitalism.

Sweezy also made major contributions to the interpretation of Marxist economic theory and to Marxist historiography. While teaching at Harvard in the early 1940s he published his classic text, *The Theory of Capitalist Development: Principles of Marxian Political Economy* (1942).[43] The book has remained one of the few fairly comprehensive studies of Marxist economics, but it was also a book of its time. Written in the context of Fascism and war in Europe, it includes explicit discussion of the connections between the later phases of capitalism and imperialism, militarism and Fascism. It also provided one of the first extended introductions for English readers of continental Marxist crisis theory. Sweezy's long-standing interest in theories of accumulation, crisis and stagnation dates from this early work.

Finally, Sweezy adopted Schumpeter's historical approaches and interests. He made an early contribution to economic history in his *Monopoly and Competition in the English Coal Trade, 1550-1850* (Harvard Economic Studies), and with his review of Maurice Dobb's *Studies in the Development of Capitalism*, he started the great Marxist debate on the transition from feudalism to capitalism.[44] His impatience with a Eurocentric Marxism structured his critique of the Western European cultural bias of Dobb's concept of feudalism. He therefore placed his explanation of the transition from feudalism on the revival of trade and the emergence of the world economy. Sweezy remembers his favourite historical writers as Pirenne and Toynbee and the immediate background to his review of Dobb's *Studies* was a reading of Pirenne's *Mohammad and Charlemagne*.[45]

II

The great political economists of this century developed their analyses and critiques of capitalism from many different perspectives and frameworks. They stand among the great dissident intellectuals of their day. But for most of them there was also a common ground of interest in the unprecedented significance of monopolistic and oligopolistic economic structures, in the dynamics of accumulation and economic crisis and in economic history.

Piero Sraffa and Joan Robinson stand apart from all the other political economists considered here. They did have some common interests with the others in the economics of imperfect competition. Sraffa's early papers of 1925–26 incorporated a section on monopoly within the general critique of Marshall's method.[46] And Joan Robinson did study Marx's reproduction schemes even before she began to write on capital and growth. It was from these that Kalecki had started his discussion of the theory of effective demand, the nature of the trade cycle, the theory of cyclical growth and the theory of effective distribution. Joan Robinson also established an apparent connection with this tradition of economic dynamics with her introduction to Rosa Luxemburg's *Accumulation of Capital* (1951 edition).[47] But Joan Robinson's interests here lay more in finding analogies between some of Luxemburg's theories and latter-day Keynesian ideas than in developing the lines of dynamic analysis arising from Luxemburg and the Austro–Marxists.[48] She was an admirer and defender of Kalecki, and she adopted the Kaleckian framework in her theory of distribution and the theory of prices in her growth models. But Piero Sraffa's and Joan Robinson's special interest in the theoretical foundations and methods of neoclassical economic theory, and with this the structure of classical and Marxist theory, paralleled the work on economic dynamics developed by others.

The other political economists included in the volume all espoused and used an historical framework for their theory and sought to develop an economic dynamics of capitalist accumulation and stagnation or crisis. Their analyses, furthermore, incorporated the monopoly phase of capitalism.

Maurice Dobb's affinities with the others were indirect — his antecedents lay much more closely in the English than continental socialist tradition. The English sources of his socialism did not mean, however, that he accepted contemporary varieties of English socialist doctrine. He did not defend the under-consumptionist revival of Hobson's theory of imperialism, nor the analysis of guild socialism or Fabian social democracy.[49] But he developed his interpretations of Marxist economics with a historian's approach, interests and framework. His early historical interests and his first research on institutional and historical aspects of the capitalist firm were not forgotten. And it is thus that Amartya Sen has ascribed to the historian's perspective Dobb's concern with the long-run fluctuations of capitalism and his emphasis on descriptive richness in Marx's economic analysis.

The other four political economists discussed here, even Schumpeter, found an important source of their inspiration in continental Marxism, especially the legacy of Rosa Luxemburg and the Austro–Marxists. Rosa Luxemburg's flawed but brilliant *magnum opus*, *The Accumulation of Capital*,[50] was an intervention in the political debate between the orthodox Marxists and the revisionists over the prospects of capitalist expansion or breakdown. Using Marx's reproduction schemes in the second volume of *Capital*, she argued that he did not demonstrate the possibility of accumulation in a closed capitalist system. A non-capitalist environment would be necessary to provide the effective demand for the realisation of surplus value and for the further accumulation of capital. The book provided both a denunciation of imperialism and a prediction of its inevitable breakdown with the eventual exhaustion of the non-capitalist environment.

Luxemburg's economic theory was flawed: there was no necessary impossibility of capital accumulation in a closed capitalist system; and she treated government expenditure as a form of realisation independent of the means of financing.[51] Yet despite these errors of economic analysis, Luxemburg produced a powerful and unified economic and political argument, whose substance certainly inspired Kalecki's, and later Sweezy's, account of the breakdown controversy.

Kalecki rehabilitated Luxemburg. He referred to her as one of

Marx's most eminent pupils.

> In her *Akkumulation des Kapitals* she stressed the point that if capitalists are saving, their profits can be 'realised' only if a corresponding amount is spent by them on investment. She, however, considered impossible the persistence of net investment (at least in the long run) in a closed capitalist economy; thus according to her it is only the existence of exports to the non-capitalist countries which allows for the expansion of the capitalist system. The theory cannot be accepted as a whole, but the necessity of covering the 'gap of saving' by home investment or exports was outlined by her perhaps more clearly than anywhere else before the publication of Mr Keynes's *General Theory*.[52]

Kalecki was also impressed with her analysis of the rise of militarism and government expenditure on armaments. He accepted her scepticism on the prospects of long-term expanded reproduction; he reached the same conclusions with different reasoning.

Luxemburg's book produced a storm of debate and criticism not just from revisionists but from other mainstream Marxists. Among these were a group later called the Austro–Marxists who took a similar long-term view of capitalist development and sought to formulate the characteristics of the later phases of capitalist development. It was in the years leading up to 1914 that Adler, Renner, Hilferding and Bauer sought to develop Marxism as an empirical social science. Politically they stood between the revisionist social democratic parties and the early established Communist parties. Their work was an important influence on Schumpeter and Sweezy and also affected Steindl.

Bauer's article 'The accumulation of capital', published in 1913 in *Die Neue Zeit*, started as a review of Rosa Luxemburg's book, but ultimately developed a sophisticated two-sector growth model which went much further than Marx's treatment of extended reproduction in Volume II of *Capital*.[53] Hilferding's classic, *Finance Capital* (1923), was also concerned with the circulation and process of capitalist production. But Hilferding sought to develop Marx's analysis to understand the later phases of capitalism. He therefore emphasised the theory of money, the growth of joint stock companies and the restriction of competition by cartels, economic crises and imperialism. Hilferding argued that a structural change had occurred in capitalism with the merging of banking and industrial capital which had produced what he termed 'finance capital'. He argued that the rise in the organic composition of capital and the fall in the profit rate made competition too expensive. Cartels, trusts and monopolies also entailed state intervention and imperialist policies. He observed the trend to central planning encouraged by the needs of the war economy and from this coined the term 'organised capitalism'. Hilferding agreed with Luxemburg in defining finance capital and imperialism as the final stages of capitalism. But Hilferding was less hopeful of inevitable economic breakdown.[54]

Schumpeter acknowledged at several points his debts to the Austro–Marxists. In his essay on imperialism he gave credit to Bauer and Hilferding for demonstrating the connections between protection, imperialism and the formation of cartels. He dealt in some detail with the Austro–Marxists in *Capitalism, Socialism and Democracy* and in *Business Cycles* he referred to Renner's concept of 'social imperialism' as nearer the truth than his own theory.[55]

Schumpeter's debt to the Austro–Marxists, however, went much deeper than this. His concept of 'trustified capitalism' and his analysis of its implications for capitalist development had very close parallels to Hilferding's analysis. He wrote of 'trustified capitalism': 'Innovation is, in this case, not anymore embodied *typically* in new firms, but goes on within the big units now existing, largely independent of individual persons'. Specialists instead of leaders and individual initiative took over. The causes of capitalist instability inherent in the individual entrepreneur were, he thought, disappearing.

> Capitalism, whilst economically stable, and even gaining in stability, creates by rationalising the human mind, a mentality and style of life incompatible with its own fundamental conditions, motives and social institutions, and will be changed, although not by economic necessity and probably even at some sacrifice of economic welfare into an order of things which it will not be merely a matter of taste and terminology to call it socialism or not.[56]

Sweezy's debt to the Austro–Marxists, as well as to Kalecki and Steindl, is obvious throughout his work. A large part of his early work, *The Theory of Capitalist Development*, is devoted to substantial sections on 'Crises and depressions' and 'Imperialism', and the work of Luxemburg and her critics and Hilferding is carefully considered. Sweezy regarded himself as part of the tradition of Marxism which he termed 'neo-Marxism' which dealt with both monopoly capital and capitalist dynamics. He aligned his work with that of Hilferding, Luxemburg, Lenin, Kalecki and Steindl.[57] He was for a long time fascinated by theories of capitalist crisis and stagnation and acknowledged that conventional economics had done some important work on this.

The vision of capitalist stagnation emanating from *The General Theory* was, he argued, followed up by only one of Keynes's disciples, Hansen, who developed a theory of the tendency to stagnation. Hansen had explained the stagnation of the 1930s by the decline of investment opportunities which was not compensated for by a proportionate decline in the propensity to save. He traced these lower investment opportunities to reductions in the rate of population increase, the closing of the frontier and the higher capital-saving bias of new technologies. And he argued that left to itself, the system would stagnate. Schumpeter, too, produced a theory of stagnation, one which placed the anti-capitalist politics of the New Deal in the role of villain of the piece. But it was Steindl he credited with providing the first full-scale analysis of stagnation by constructing this around Kalecki's concept of the 'degree of monopoly'.[58]

The focus of the Austro–Marxists on developing Marxism as an empirical social science, and the historical materialism of Rosa Luxemburg's work, form both a direct and indirect framework for the particular approach to political economy taken by Dobb, Kalecki, Steindl, Schumpeter and Sweezy. Their work attempted to develop economic principles which would account for the effects of the monopolistic and imperialist features of contemporary capitalism. It also sought to analyse capitalism as a process: these writers analysed the dynamics, the fluctuations and the transformation of the capitalist system.

The place of history in the approach of this political economy was eloquently declared by both Schumpeter and Sweezy. Schumpeter opened his chapter on 'The techniques of economic analysis' in his monumental *History of Economic Analysis* (1954) with the statement: 'What distinguishes the scientific economists from all other people who think, talk and write about economic topics is a command of techniques that we class under three heads: history, statistics and "theory". The three together make up what we call economic analysis.'

> Of these fundamental fields, economic history — which issues into and includes present day facts — is by far the most important. I wish to state right now that if, starting my work afresh I were told that I could study only one of these three but could have my choice, it would be economic history that I should choose.

Sweezy, repeating these words in 1971, added 'I personally believe this to be one of the wisest and most profound, as well as most neglected, of Schumpeter's teachings'. He argued that economic history interpreted in the broad sense 'would not only have to be restored to the position it occupied forty or fifty years ago, but elevated far above it ... it would have to be made the centrepiece of the curriculum'.[59] Even Joan Robinson, who rarely made explicit use of historical analyses, always stressed in a general way the over-riding importance of history.[60]

The political economists whose lives and work are discussed in this book were intellectuals and scholars, attributes rarely found in economists. Their approach to economics was one which linked theoretical insight to concern for contemporary policy and the real world, and to considerable historical learning. Dissident though they were, their impact on, and example to, their generation was profound. But, sadly, their generation is passing, and academic economics now has no room for the critical spirit. Professional it may be; but academic economics is now conducted within a dramatically narrowed scope, lacking fundamental self-criticism and the passion for social change.

Notes

1. See John Vaizey, 'Keynes and Cambridge', Robert Skidelsky, 'The political meaning of the Keynesian revolution' and Stuart Holland, 'Keynes and the socialists', in Robert Skidelsky (ed.), *The End of the Keynesian Era: Essays on the Disintegration of Keynesian Political Economy*, Macmillan, 1977.
2. G.R. Feiwel, *The Intellectual Capital of Michal Kalecki*, University of Tennessee Press, 1975, p.72.
3. See Joan Robinson, 'The theory of normal prices and reconstruction of economic theory', in G.R. Feiwel, *Issues in Contemporary Macroeconomics and Distribution*, Macmillan, 1985, p. 157.
4. Eprime Eshag, 'Kalecki's political economy in comparison with Keynes', in Michal Kalecki Memorial Issue, *Oxford Bulletin of Economics and Statistics*, vol. 39, no. 1, 1977, p. 81.

5. See Feiwel, *Intellectual Capital*, p. 72.
6. Joan Robinson, 'The theory of normal prices', p. 157. Alternatively, the combination of both approaches is apparent in the work of those such as Abba Lerner, who accepted both socialism and the tenets of microeconomic theory. His *Economics of Control* (1944) combined marginal analysis with the new macroeconomics. See Irwin Sorrel, 'Abba Petachya Lerner 1903–1982: six decades of achievement', *Journal of Post Keynesian Economics*, vol. 6, no. 1, 1983, p. 11.
7. Feiwel, *Intellectual Capital*, p. 54.
8. Elizabeth Durbin, *New Jerusalem: The Labour Party and the Economics of Democratic Socialism*, Routledge, 1985, pp. 13, 149.
9. Nicholas Kaldor, 'Piero Sraffa', *Cambridge Journal of Economics*, vol. 8, no. 1, 1984, p. 5.
10. Ian Steedman, *Marx After Sraffa*, New Left Books, 1977, p. 13.
11. G.C. Harcourt, 'The end of an era: Joan Robinson (1903–1983) and Piero Sraffa (1898–1983)', *Journal of Post Keynesian Economics*, vol. 6, no. 3, 1984, p. 467.
12. See for example, Steedman, *Marx After Sraffa*.
13. G.C. Harcourt, 'On the contributions of Joan Robinson and Piero Sraffa to economic theory', *Economic Journal*, Supplement, Conference Proceedings, vol. 96, 1986, pp. 96–108.
14. G.C. Harcourt, 'Contributions of Robinson and Sraffa', p. 98.
15. These are collected in vols 3, 4 and 5 of her *Collected Economic Papers*, Blackwell, 1951–79.
16. See his 1925 LSE MA thesis, *Capitalist Enterprise and Social Progress*.
17. See Maurice Dobb, 'Random biographical notes', *Cambridge Journal of Economics*, vol. 2, no. 2, 1978, p. 119.
18. Dobb, 'Random notes', p. 119.
19. In M.H. Dobb, *Political Economy and Capitalism: Some Essays in Economic Tradition*, Routledge, 1973. The remainder of this paragraph is based on material in Amartya Sen's lecture on Dobb at the University of Warwick, 1986.
20. See Amartya Sen, 'On the labour theory of value: some methodological issues', *Cambridge Journal of Economics*, vol. 2, 1978, pp. 184-185.
21. M.H. Dobb, *Theories of Value and Distribution since Adam Smith: Ideology and Economic Theory*, Cambridge University Press, 1973.
22. Cited in R.L. Meek, 'Obituary of Maurice Dobb', in *The Proceedings of the British Academy*, vol. 53, 1978.
23. A.K. Sen, 'Maurice Herbert Dobb,' in J. Eatwell, Murray Milgate, Peter Newman (eds), *The New Palgrave Dictionary of Economics*, Macmillan, 1987, pp. 910-912. Other points in this paragraph have been drawn from Amartya Sen's lecture on Dobb, University of Warwick, 1986.
24. Tadeusz Kowalik, 'The institutional framework of Dobb's economics', *Cambridge Journal of Economics*, vol. 2, 1978, pp. 141-151.

25. Robert Brenner, 'Dobb on the transition from feudalism to capitalism', *Cambridge Journal of Economics*, vol. 2, 1978, pp. 121-140.
26. Josef Steindl, 'A personal portrait of Michal Kalecki', *Journal of Post Keynesian Economics*, vol. 3, no. 4, 1981, pp. 590-597; and Edward Lipinski, 'Michal Kalecki', *Oxford Bulletin of Economics and Statistics*, Michael Kalecki Memorial Issue, vol. 39, no. 1, 1977, p. 74.
27. Eshag, 'Kalecki's political economy in comparison with Keynes', p. 81.
28. Peter Kriesler, *Kalecki's Microanalysis*, Cambridge University Press, 1987, p. 51.
29. Eshag, 'Introduction', p. 3; G.D.N. Worswick, 'Kalecki at Oxford', p. 20; W. Brus, 'Kalecki's economics of socialism', pp. 59–66; I. Sachs, 'Kalecki and development planning', p. 48, all in Kalecki Memorial Issue, *Oxford Bulletin*.
30. See Steindl, 'Personal portrait of Michal Kalecki', p. 593; Joan Robinson, 'Michal Kalecki on the economics of capitalism', Kalecki Memorial Issue, *Oxford Bulletin*, pp. 10–11 and Feiwel, *Intellectual Capital*, p. 72.
31. Robinson, 'Michal Kalecki on the economics of capitalism', p. 16.
32. J. Steindl, *Maturity and Stagnation in American Capitalism*, Basil Blackwell, 1952 (reprinted by Monthly Review Press, 1976).
33. See J. Steindl, 'Stagnation theory and stagnation policy', *Cambridge Journal of Economics*, vol. 3, no. 1, 1979, p. 7.
34. J.A. Schumpeter, *The Theory of Economic Development: An Inquiry into Profits, Capital, Credit, Interest and the Business Cycle*, Oxford University Press, 1961, p. x.
35. See P.M. Sweezy, 'Introduction', in J.A. Schumpeter, *Imperialism and Social Classes*, Oxford University Press, 1951, p. ix.
36. See J.A. Schumpeter, 'Capitalism in the postwar world', in R.V. Clemence, *Essays of J.A. Schumpeter*, Addison-Wesley, 1951, p. 173; Sweezy, 'Introduction', p. ix; J.A. Schumpeter, 'The instability of capitalism', *Economic Journal*, vol. 38, no. 151, 1928, p. 383; and J.A. Schumpeter, *Imperialism and Social Classes*, Basil Blackwell, 1951, p. ix.
37. Schumpeter, 'Capitalism in the postwar world', p. 176; see also, *The Theory of Economic Development*, pp. 93–94, and Sweezy, 'Introduction', p. xvi.
38 See T.B. Bottomore, 'The decline of capitalism sociologically considered', in Arnold Heertje, *Schumpeter's Vision of Capitalism, Socialism and Democracy after 40 years*, Praeger, 1981, pp. 22–45.
39. P.M. Sweezy, 'Introduction', pp. vii and xxii.
40. Editorial, 'Twenty-five eventful years', *Monthly Review*, vol. 26, no. 2, 1974, p. 5; P.M. Sweezy, 'The theory of monopoly capitalism', *Monthly Review*, vol. 23, no. 11, 1972, pp. 12–15.

41. P.A. Baran and P.M. Sweezy, *Monopoly Capital: An Essay on the American Economic and Social Order*, Penguin, 1968, p. 16.
42. Sweezy, 'Theory of monopoly capitalism,' pp. 14–15. Also see P.M. Sweezy, 'Keynesian economics: the first quarter century', in P.M. Sweezy, *Modern Capitalism and Other Essays*, Monthly Review Press, 1972, p. 83.
43. P.M. Sweezy, *The Theory of Capitalist Development: Principles of Marxian Political Economy*, Dennis Dobson, London, 1946.
44. See Maurice Dobb, 'Foreword', in P.M. Sweezy, *The Theory of Capitalist Development*, p. v and David Goldaway, 'Fifty years of *Science and Society*', *Science and Society*, vol. 50, no. 3, 1986, p. 260–279.
45. P.M. Sweezy, 'Feudalism to capitalism revisited', *Science and Society*, vol. 50, no. 1, 1986, pp. 81–84.
46. Harcourt, 'Piero Sraffa and Joan Robinson', p. 27.
47. *Ibid.*, p. 100.
48. P.M. Sweezy, 'Rosa Luxemburg and the theory of capitalism', in P.M. Sweezy, *The Present as History*, Monthly Review Press, 1953, pp. 291–295.
49. See P.J. Cain, 'Hobson, Wilshire and the theory of capitalist imperialism', *History of Political Economy*, vol. 17, No. 3, 1985, pp. 455–460.
50. R. Luxemburg (translator Agnes Schwarzschild), *The Accumulation of Capital*, Routledge, 1951.
51. Sweezy, 'Rosa Luxemburg', p. 293 and Feiwel, *Intellectual Capital*, pp. 57–59.
52. M. Kalecki, *Essays in the Theory of Economic Fluctuations*, (1939), cited in Feiwel, *Intellectual Capital*, p. 56.
53. See J.E. King, 'Otto Bauer's "Accumulation of capital"', *History of Political Economy*, vol. 18, no. 1, 1986, pp. 87–110.
54. See T.B. Bottomore and Patrick Goode, *Austro–Marxism*, Oxford University Press, 1978, p. 23.
55. Bottomore and Goode, *Austro–Marxism*, p. 35 and Sweezy, 'Introduction', p. ix.
56. Joseph Schumpeter, 'The instability of capitalism', *Economic Journal*, vol. 38, no. 151, 1928, p. 383.
57. Sweezy, 'On the theory of monopoly capitalism', pp. 12–15.
58. Sweezy, 'Keynesian economics: the first quarter century', pp. 82–84.
59. Sweezy, 'Modern capitalism,' p. 4. Also see J.A. Schumpeter, *History of Economic Analysis*, Allen and Unwin, 1981, p. 12.
60. See for example, her paper, 'History versus equilibrium'.

2

*Maurice Herbert Dobb**

AMARTYA SEN

Maurice Dobb was born on 24 July 1900 in London. His father, Walter Herbert Dobb, had a draper's retail business and his mother Elsie Annie Moir came from a Scottish merchant's family. He was educated at Charterhouse, and then at Pembroke College, Cambridge, where he studied economics. This was followed by two postgraduate years at the London School of Economics, where he did his PhD on 'the entrepreneur'. The thesis formed the basis of his book *Capitalist Enterprise and Social Progress* (1925). Dobb returned to Cambridge at the end of 1924 on being appointed as a Lecturer in Economics. He taught in Cambridge until his retirement in 1967. He was a Fellow of Trinity College and was elected to a University Readership in 1959. He received honorary degrees from the Charles University of Prague, the University of Budapest and Leicester University, and was elected a Fellow of the British Academy. After retirement he and his wife, Barbara, stayed on in the neighbouring village of Fulbourn. He died on 17 August 1976.

Maurice Dobb was undoubtedly one of the outstanding political economists of this century. He was a Marxist and was one of the most creative contributors to Marxian economics. As Ronald Meek put it, in his obituary of Dobb for the British Academy, 'over a period of fifty years [Dobb] established and maintained his position

*This article is reprinted by kind permission of Macmillan Press Reference Books from *The New Palgrave: A Dictionary of Economics*, edited by John Eatwell, Murray Milgate and Peter Newman (London: Macmillan Press; New York: Stockton Press 1987).

as one of the most eminent Marxist economists in the world'. Dobb's *Political Economy and Capitalism* (1937) and *Studies in the Development of Capitalism* (1946) are his two most outstanding contributions to Marxist economics. The former is primarily concerned with economic theory (including such subjects as value theory, economic crises, imperialism, socialist economies) and the latter with economic history (particularly the emergence of capitalism from feudalism). These two fields — economic theory and economic history — were intimately connected in Dobb's approach to economics.

He also wrote an influential book on Soviet economic development. This was first published under the title *Russian Economic Development since the Revolution* (1928), and later in a revised edition as *Soviet Economic Development since 1917* (1948).

Throughout his life Maurice Dobb was deeply concerned with economic policy and planning. His foundational critique of 'market socialism', as developed by Oskar Lange and Abba Lerner, appeared in *The Economic Journal* of 1933, later reproduced along with a number of related contributions in his *On Economic Theory and Socialism* (1955). In later years Dobb was much concerned with planning for economic development. In three lectures delivered at the Delhi School of Economics, later published as *Some Aspects of Economic Development* (1951), Dobb discussed some of the central issues of development planning for an economy with unemployed or underutilised labour and his ideas were more extensively developed in his later book, *An Essay on Economic Growth and Planning* (1960).

Maurice Dobb also published a number of papers on more traditional fields in economic theory, including welfare economics, and some of these papers were collected together in his *Welfare Economics and the Economics of Socialism* (1969). In his *Theories of Value and Distribution since Adam Smith: Ideology and Economic Theory* (1973), he responded *inter alia* to the new developments in Cambridge political economy, including the influential *Prelude to a Critique of Economic Theory* by Piero Sraffa (1960). Maurice Dobb's association with Piero Sraffa extended over a long period, both as a colleague at Trinity College and also as a collaborator in editing *Works and Correspondence of David Ricardo*, published in eleven volumes between 1951 and 1973 (on this collaboration see Pollitt 1985).

In addition to academic writings, Maurice Dobb produced a great deal of popular writing, both for workers' education and for general public discussion. He wrote a number of pamphlets, including *The Development of Modern Capitalism* (1922), *Money and Prices* (1924), *An Outline of European History* (1926), *Modern Capitalism* (1927), *On Marxism Today* (1932), *Planning and Capitalism* (1937), *Soviet Planning and Labour in Peace and War* (1942), *Marx as an Economist: An Essay* (1943), *Capitalism Yesterday and Today* (1958), *Economic Growth and Underdeveloped Countries* (1963) and many others. Dobb was a superb communicator and the nature of his own research was much influenced by policy debates and public discussions. Dobb the economist was not only close to Dobb the historian, but also in constant company of Dobb the member of the public. It would be difficult to find another economist who could match Dobb in his extraordinary combination of genuinely highbrow theory, on the one hand, and popular writing on the other. The author of *Political Economy and Capitalism* (from the appearance of which — as Ronald Meek rightly notes — 'future historians of economic thought will probably date the emergence of Marxist economics as a really serious economic discipline') also put a good deal of effort into writing pamphlets and material for labour education and straightforward journalism. It is not possible to appreciate fully Maurice Dobb's contributions to economics without taking note of his view of the role of economics in public discussions and debates.

Another issue of importance in understanding Dobb's approach to economics is his adherence to the labour theory of value. The labour theory has been under attack not only from neoclassical economists, but also from such anti-neoclassical political economists as Joan Robinson and, indirectly, even Piero Sraffa. In his last major work, *Theories of Value and Distribution since Adam Smith* (1973), Maurice Dobb emphasises his support for the relevance of Sraffa's (1960) major contribution, which eschews the use of labour values (on this see Steedman 1977) but without abandoning his insistence on the importance of the labour theory of value. It is easy to think that there is some inconsistency here and it is tempting to trace the origin of this alleged inconsistency to Dobb's earlier writings, which made Abram Bergson remark that 'in Dobb's analysis the labour theory is not so much an analytic tool as excess baggage' (Bergson 1949, p. 445).

The key to understanding Dobb's attitude to the labour theory of value is to recognise that he did not see it just as an intermediate product in explaining relative prices and distributions. He took 'the labour-principle' as 'making an important qualitative statement about the nature of the economic problem' (Dobb 1937, p. 21). He rejected seeing the labour theory of value as simply a 'first approximation' containing 'nothing essential that cannot be expressed equally well and easily in other terms' (Dobb 1973, pp. 148–149). The description of the production process in terms of labour involvement has an interest that extends far beyond the role of the labour value magnitudes in providing a 'first approximation' for relative prices. As Dobb (1973) put it:

> there is something in the first approximation that is lacking in later approximations or cannot be expressed so easily in those terms (e.g. the first approximation may be a device for emphasising and throwing into relief something of greater generality and less particularity) [pp. 148–149].

Any description of reality involves some selection of facts to emphasise certain features and to underplay others, and the labour theory of value was seen by Dobb as emphasising the role of those who are involved in 'personal participation in the process of production *per se*' in contrast with those who do not have such personal involvement.

> As such, 'exploitation' is neither something 'metaphysical' nor simply an ethical judgement (still less 'just a noise') as has sometimes been depicted: it is a factual description of a socio-economic relationship, as much as is Marc Bloch's apt characterisation of Feudalism as a system where feudal Lords 'lived on the labour of other men' [Dobb 1973, p. 145].

The possibility of calculating prices without going through value magnitudes, and the greater efficiency of doing that (on this see Steedman 1977), does not affect this descriptive relevance of the labour theory of value in any way. Maurice Dobb also outlined the relationship of this primarily descriptive interpretation of labour theory of value with evaluative questions, e.g. assessing the 'rights of ownership' (see especially Dobb 1937).

The importance for Dobb of descriptive relevance is brought out also by his complex attitude to the utility theory of value. While he rejected the view that the utility picture is the best way of seeing relative values ('by taking as its foundation a fact of individual consciousness'), he lamented the descriptive impoverishment that is brought about by replacing the subjective utility theory by the 'revealed preference' approach.

> If all that is postulated is simply that men *choose*, without anything being stated even as to how they choose or what governs their choice, it would seem impossible for economics to provide us with any more than a sort of algebra of human choice [Dobb 1937, p. 171].

Indeed, as early as 1929, a long time before the 'revealed preference theory' was formally inaugurated by Paul Samuelson, Dobb had warned:

> Actually the whole tendency of modern theory is to abandon such psychological conceptions: to make utility and disutility coincident with observed offers in the market; to abandon a 'theory of value' in pursuit of a 'theory of price'. But this is to surrender, not to solve the problem [Dobb 1929, p. 32].

Maurice Dobb's open-minded attitude to non-Marxian traditions in economics added strength and reach to his own Marxist theorising. He could combine Marxist reasoning and methodology with other traditions and he was eager to be able to communicate with economists belonging to other schools. Dobb's honesty and lack of dogmatism were important for the development of the Marxist economic tradition in the English-speaking world because he occupied a unique position in Marxist thinking in Britain. As Eric Hobsbawm has noted, 'for several generations (as these are measured in the brief lives of students) he was not just the only Marxist economist in a British university of whom most people had heard, but virtually the only don known as a communist to the wider world' (Hobsbawm 1967, p. 1). The Marxist economic tradition was well served by Maurice Dobb's willingness to engage in spirited but courteous debates with economists of other schools. Dobb achieved this without compromising the integrity of his position. The distinctly Marxist quality of his economic writings was as important as his willingness to listen and dispassionately analyse the claims of other schools of thought with which he engaged in systematic disputation. The gentleness of Dobb's style of disputation arose from strength rather than weakness.

Dobb's willingness to appreciate positive elements in other

economic traditions while retaining the distinctive qualities of his own approach is brought out very clearly in his far-reaching critique of the theory of socialist pricing as presented by Lange, Lerner, Dickinson and others in the 1930s. Dobb noted the efficiency advantages of a price mechanism, especially in a static context. He was, however, one of the first economists to analyse clearly the conflict between the demands of efficiency expressed in the equilibrium conditions of the Lange–Lerner price mechanism (and also, of course, in a perfectly competitive market equilibrium) and the demands that would be imposed by the requirements of equality, given the initial conditions. In his paper titled 'Economic theory and the problems of a socialist economy' published in 1933, Maurice Dobb argued thus:

> If carpenters are scarcer or more costly to train than scavengers, the market will place a higher value upon their services, and carpenters will derive a higher income and have greater 'voting power' as consumers. On the side of supply the extra 'costliness' of carpenters will receive expression, but only at the expense of giving carpenters a differential 'pull' as consumers, and hence vitiating the index of demand. On the other hand, if carpenters and scavengers are to be given equal weight as consumers by assuring them equal incomes, then the extra costliness of carpenters will find no expression in costs of production. Here is the central dilemma. Precisely because consumers are also producers, both costs and needs are precluded from receiving simultaneous expression in the same system of market valuations. Precisely to the extent that market valuations are rendered adequate in one direction they lose significance in the other [Dobb 1933, p. 37].

The fact that, given an initial distribution of resources, the demands of efficiency and those of equity may — and typically will — conflict is, of course, one of the major issues in the theory of resource allocation, with implications for market socialism as well as for competitive markets in a private ownership economy. As a matter of fact, Marx had *inter alia* noted this conflict in his *Critique of Gotha Programme*, but in the discussion centring around Lange–Lerner systems, this deep conflict had attracted relatively little attention, except in the arguments presented by Maurice Dobb. The fact that even a socialist economy has to cope with inequalities of initial resource distribution (arising from, among other things, differences in inherited talents and acquired skills) makes it a relevant question for a socialist economy as well as for a competitive market economy, and Dobb's was one of the first clear analyses of this central question of resource allocation.

The second respect in which Maurice Dobb found the literature on market socialism inadequate concerns allocation over time. In discussing the achievements and failures of the market mechanism, Maurice Dobb argued that the planning of investment decisions 'may contribute much more to human welfare than could the most perfect micro-economic adjustment, of which the market (if it worked like the textbooks, at least, and there were no income-inequalities) is admittedly more fitted in most cases to take care' (Dobb 1960, p. 76). In his book *An Essay in Economic Growth and Planning* (1960), Dobb provided a major investigation of the basis of planned investment decisions, covering overall investment rates, sectoral divisions, choice of techniques and pricing policies related to allocation (including that over time).

Dobb's contribution here relates closely to his analysis of the problems of economic development. In his earlier book *Some Aspects of Economic Development* (1951), Dobb had already presented a pioneering analysis of the problem of economic development in a surplus labour economy, with shortage of capital and of many skills. While, on the one hand, he anticipated W. A. Lewis's better-known investigation of economic growth with 'unlimited supplies of labour', he also went on to demonstrate the far-reaching implications of the overall savings rates being socially suboptimal and inadequate. Briefly, he showed that this requires not only policies directly aimed at raising the rates of saving and investment, but that it also has implications for the choice of techniques, sectoral balances and price fixation.

In a brief note, it is not possible to do justice to the enormous range of Maurice Dobb's contributions to economic theory, applied economics and economic history. Different authors influenced by Maurice Dobb have emphasised different aspects of his many-sided works (see, for example, Feinstein (ed.) 1967 and Maurice Dobb Memorial Issue 1978). He has also had influence even outside professional economics, particularly in history especially through his analysis of the development of capitalism (Dobb 1946, 1950).

It is worth emphasising that aside from the explicit contributions made by Maurice Dobb to economic history, he also used a historical approach to economic analysis in general. Maurice

Dobb's deep concern for descriptive richness (as exemplified by his analysis of 'the requirements of a theory of value'), his insistence on not neglecting the long-run features of resource allocation (influencing his work on planning as well as development), his concern with observed phenomena in slumps and depressions in examining theories of 'crises', and so on, all relate to the historian's perspective. Dobb's works in the apparently divergent areas of economic theory, applied economics and economic history are, in fact, quite closely related to each other.

Maurice Dobb was not only a major bridge builder between Marxist and non-Marxist economic traditions (aside from pioneering the development of Marxist economics in Britain and to some extent in the entire English-speaking world), he also built many bridges between the different pursuits of economic theorists, applied economists and economic historians. Dobb's political economy involved the rejection of the narrowly economic as well as the narrowly doctrinaire. He was a great economist in the best of the broad tradition of classical political economy.

References

Bergson, A. (1949) 'Socialist economics', in H.S. Ellis, *A Survey of Contemporary Economics*, Blakiston.

Dobb, M.H. (1925) *Capitalist Enterprise and Social Progress*, Routledge.

Dobb, M.H. (1928) *Russian Economic Development since the Revolution*, Routledge.

Dobb, M.H. (1929) 'A sceptical view of the theory of wages', *Economic Journal*, vol. 39.

Dobb, M.H. (1933) 'Economic theory and the problems of a socialist economy', *Economic Journal*, vol. 43.

Dobb, M.H. (1937) *Political Economy and Capitalism: Some Essays in Economic Tradition*, Routledge.

Dobb, M.H. (1946) *Studies in the Development of Capitalism*, Routledge.

Dobb, M.H. (1950) 'Comments on Professor H.K. Takahashi's "Transformation from feudalism to capitalism"', *Science and Society*, vol. 14.

Dobb, M.H. (1951) *Some Aspects of Economic Development: Three Lectures*, Ranjit Publishers for the Delhi School of Economics.

Dobb, M.H. (1955) *On Economic Theory and Socialism*, Routledge.

Dobb, M.H. (1960) *An Essay on Economic Growth and Planning*, Routledge.

Dobb, M.H. (1969) *Welfare Economics and the Economics of Socialism*, Cambridge University Press.

Dobb, M.H. (1973) *Theories of Value and Distribution since Adam Smith : Ideology and Economic Theory*, Cambridge University Press.

Feinstein (ed.), C. (1967) *Socialism, Capitalism and Economic Growth : Essays Presented to Maurice Dobb*, Cambridge University Press.

Hobsbawm, E.J. (1967) 'Maurice Dobb', in C. Feinstein (ed.) *Socialism, Capitalism and Economic Growth : Essays Presented to Maurice Dobb*, Cambridge University Press.

Maurice Dobb Memorial Issue (1978) *Cambridge Journal of Economics*, vol. 2.

Meek, R. (1978) 'Obituary of Maurice Herbert Dobb', in *The Proceedings of the British Academy 1977*, vol. 53.

Pollitt, B.H. (1985) 'Clearing the path for *Production of Commodities by Means of Commodities* : notes on the collaboration of Maurice Dobb in Piero Sraffa's edition of the *Works and Correspondence of David Ricardo*', mimeographed.

Sraffa, P. (1960) *Production of Commodities by Means of Commodities : Prelude to a Critique of Economic Theory*, Cambridge University Press.

Sraffa, P. with the collaboration of M.H. Dobb (1951-73) *Works and Correspondence of David Ricardo*, 11 volumes, Cambridge University Press.

Steedman, I. (1977) *Marx after Sraffa*, NLB.

3

*On the Contributions of Joan Robinson and Piero Sraffa to Economic Theory**

G. C. HARCOURT

I thank, but in no way implicate, Tom Asimakopulos, Andrea Boitani, Lilia Costablile, Sukhamoy Chakravarty, Phyllis Deane, Meghnad Desai, Keith Frearson, John Hatch, Jan Kregel, Peter Kriesler, Michael Lawson, Terry O'Shaughnessy, Ian Steedman and Michael White for their comments on a draft of an earlier version of this essay, and Maxine Berg for helpful guidelines on how to restructure the earlier version for this volume.

I

Joan Robinson and Piero Sraffa died within a month of each other in 1983. Sraffa, who was born in August 1898, was five years older than Joan Robinson; they had known one another for over fifty years.

---

*This essay is based on two earlier versions. One appeared in G.C. Harcourt (1986) 'On the influence of Piero Sraffa on the contributions of Joan Robinson to economic theory', *Economic Journal*, Supplement, vol. 96, pp. 96-108. The other appeared in O.F. Hamouda (ed.) (1986) *Controversies in Political Economy : Selected Essays of G.C. Harcourt*, Wheatsheaf.

Joan Robinson had attended Sraffa's lectures in Cambridge in the late 1920s and they were colleagues in the Faculty of Economics and Politics from 1933 on when Joan Robinson was appointed to an Assistant Lectureship. Sraffa himself had been appointed to a teaching post in 1927 but, as Austin Robinson (1977, p.29) recalls, in 1930 he begged to be taken off teaching. He retained the post of Marshall Librarian and soon after resigning his lectureship, the post of mentor to the research students was created for him. This allowed him to work on the Ricardo volumes and it relieved him of the anxieties which teaching, especially the critical destruction of the arguments of people whose work he admired (Marshall, for example), caused him.

Joan Robinson's first major work, *The Economics of Imperfect Competition* (1933), was inspired by the 'pregnant suggestion' in Sraffa's 1926 *Economic Journal* article concerning the generality of monopoly rather than competition as the way forward in the theory of value. They were both part of the small group of exceptional young people who constituted the 'circus' which in the early 1930s argued out the *Treatise* and discussed with Keynes (through the Messenger Angel from the Gods, Richard Kahn (J.M. Keynes 1973, p. 339) the emerging questions to be tackled and the arguments of the *General Theory*.

Joan Robinson remained an ardent Keynesian though she was increasingly to adopt the structure by which Kalecki independently discovered the principal contribution of the *General Theory*. If we may judge from the written record (but let us not do a Patinkin),[1] Sraffa was to distance himself more and more from the Keynes of the *General Theory*. Partly this may have been because he conceived of his own project of the revival of classical political economy, especially of the concept of the surplus as the core of the theory of value and distribution, as both at a higher level of abstraction and as dealing with more fundamental or, at least, more basic issues. To someone who was deeply influenced by the whole corpus of the work of Ricardo and Marx (and of Marshall), whose interest was more in the class struggle and the notion of internal contradictions, Keynes's solution of the realisation problem inevitably must have seemed to have been of relatively narrow scope even if of profound practical importance in the aftermath of a deep depression. (It is certainly possible to sense a similar attitude towards Keynes from Maurice Dobb, who was later to be Sraffa's collaborator on the Ricardo volumes.) Partly also Sraffa may have been unhappy with the use which Keynes made of Sraffa's construct of own rates of interest in Chapter 17 of the *General Theory*. Sraffa (1932) employed the construct to criticise from within the argument of Hayek's *Prices and Production* rather than to provide an integral part of a positive theory of the operation of capitalist markets.

Joan Robinson's *magnum opus*, *The Accumulation of Capital* (1956), was also much influenced by Sraffa's contributions, this time his remarkable introduction to volume I of the Ricardo work (Sraffa with Dobb 1951). Here he set out the first major step of his attempt to revive the surplus approach of the classical economists which had 'been submerged and forgotten since the advent of the "marginal" method' (Sraffa 1960, p.v). And, of course, when Sraffa's own *magnum opus*, a slim volume of less than a hundred pages, was published in 1960, Joan Robinson wrote one of the most perceptive reviews of it (1965a (1961)) and joined forces with Sraffa in a combined attack on the orthodox theory of value and distribution. For a while they were as one, detecting in the capital-reversing and reswitching results the Achilles heel of orthodoxy and arguing that the theory of profits in capitalist economies was to be found in the surplus approach. But towards the end of their lives they were to disagree on what was most damaging to their mutual opponents; Joan Robinson shifted the emphasis of her attack to one on methods rather than particular results while Sraffa or, at least, the Sraffians, concentrated on the results obtained within a particular methodology. The latter, it was argued, had been common to economic theory from the classical political economists to Hicks's *Value and Capital*, or, at least, until Hayek's work in the late 1920s. Hayek sensed the inconsistencies associated with the concept of capital within the supply and demand framework which were made explicit in the 1960s and responded by changing both the questions asked and the equilibrium used (see Milgate 1979, Garegnani 1976).

Sraffa was a great intellectual influence on Joan Robinson; it is also clear from those parts of their correspondence which have survived[2] that they were extremely close friends who had great affection for each other and cared very much about the other's wellbeing. Much of the correspondence consists of the intimate discussion of close friends who share a common language and who enjoy gossip; but it also includes some fascinating debates, in which Sraffa invariably emerges as the winner. In this battle of champions even

Joan Robinson's renowned logic and insights had to give way to Sraffa's quite remarkable powers of criticism and illumination. He could take what seemed to be a neat and powerful definition or contrast and show that it was empty of meaning. This was done without rancour and with affection and wry humour. Even as one's head came off the sensation was as much one of amusement as of amazement; there was certainly no immediate pain. Sraffa's own self-mockery and sense of irony were much in evidence, especially in the letters in which he discusses whether he should accept a fellowship at Trinity which had become available because D.H. Robertson had left Cambridge for a Chair in London.

Joan Robinson continued to work into the last year of her life. She gave the prestigious Tanner Lectures at Utah in 1981 and two of her last papers were substantial contributions: 'Spring cleaning' (1985 (1980)), where among other things she summed up where she stood with regard to Sraffa's contributions in particular and economic theory in general; and a paper (with Frank Wilkinson 1985 (1983)) on ideology and logic, a major preoccupation throughout her life. 'Spring cleaning' and its aftermath left her near despair, feeling that she had been discussing economic theory for over fifty years and that it had come to pieces in her hands; an almost nihilistic conclusion, typically harsh and honest but too hard on herself and her achievements. Gram and Walsh (1983) give a more hopeful account of them and the promise which they hold for workers in the future.

Sraffa was in ill health for much of the last ten years of his life. While he was still able to discuss issues which excited him he did not write anything after the publication of *Production of Commodities* (1960) and the few postscripts to it (the reply to Harrod, for example, 1962), though he gave considerable help to the many serious and devoted scholars who came to see him. It should be stressed that Sraffa was much more of a 'loner' than Joan Robinson, at ease with his own company and in thinking issues through, though he did, of course, take part in discussions and welcomed the company of congenial minds. Joan Robinson, by contrast, liked to discuss and to exchange written comments. For many years she went on long weekend walks with Richard Kahn and others, including Sraffa, in order to thrash out problems in economic theory and she used to circulate drafts of her papers regularly and to correspond with people on issues. While Joan Robinson was generally a fearless person, handing it out without fear or favour, she held Sraffa in awe and was wary of arousing his wrath. (No one can blame her for *that* — see Austin Robinson (1977, p. 29) and Harcourt (1984a, p. 468).)

II

Piero Sraffa had a major influence on the intellectual developments of the twentieth century. He was an intimate friend of Antonio Gramsci, Keynes and Ludwig Wittgenstein and played an important part in changing Wittgenstein's philosophical views between the *Tractatus* (1922) and the *Philosophical Investigations* (1953). Sraffa was the most important critic of the orthodox theory of value and distribution in the twentieth century. Yet though he was to make outstanding contributions to pure theory, about the rigour and coherence of which he had well-defined ideas (see, for example Sraffa 1961, pp. 305–306), the object of his theorising always had a political and social aspect.

From his school days he had taken a keen interest in political issues and early on became a socialist. He fought in the Italian army during World War I and, as a result of his experiences, became a pacifist. He opposed Mussolini's Fascist regime; his friendship with Gramsci came about because of this. Even in his earliest economic work — his dissertation *L'inflazione monetaria in Italia durante e dopo la guerra* (1920) — important political, institutional and sociological ingredients were already present. And though the analytical structure was the then dominant form of the quantity theory of money, Sraffa's own particular contribution was to integrate the sociological and institutional determinants of wages and employment into this framework. He incurred the wrath of Mussolini by exposing the corrupt practices of the pre-Fascist and Fascist state with regard to the private banking system in his 1922 *Economic Journal* and *Manchester Guardian* articles on the bank crisis in Italy. It was his interest in monetary matters that first attracted Keynes's attention and while they were later to follow different lines of research in economics, their friendship remained as close as ever, not least because they were both passionate bibliophiles. Sraffa translated Keynes's *A Tract on Monetary Reform* into Italian in 1925.

In the mid-1920s, at Gramsci's suggestion, Sraffa commenced a study and then a critique of the orthodox theory of value and distribution. First, in Sraffa 1925) and Sraffa (1926), he attacked the partial equilibrium analysis of Marshall and then, later, the general equilibrium framework, all different examples of the dominant supply and demand theories. As a challenge to these theories, Sraffa also spawned the imperfect competition revolution which others were to develop (in a manner probably not to his liking).

Sraffa's 1925 and 1926 articles (the first six or seven pages of the second article are a lucid summary of the argument of the first paper) are attacks on the logical foundations of Marshall's theory of competitive value. That theory depends upon 'the fundamental symmetry existing between the forces of supply and demand', using the method of partial equilibrium — Sraffa calls it 'particular equilibrium' (1926, p.539) — so that 'the essential causes determining the price of particular commodities may be ... grouped together so as to be represented by a pair of intersecting curves of collective demand and supply' (1926, p. 535). Sraffa's conclusion is that the only case which is logically consistent with the approach is one of constant costs: 'In normal cases the cost of production of commodities produced competitively ... must be regarded as constant in respect of small variations in the quantity produced' (1926, pp. 540–541). Moreover, as Sraffa adds in a footnote (note 1, p. 541), the constancy arises from 'the absence of causes which tend to cause the cost either to increase or diminish' and not from an improbable 'accidental balancing of two opposite tendencies', as Sidgwick and Marshall would have it. In which case, we are back with the discredited classical theory of value which the demand and supply theories, together with the subjective theory of value and the marginal method, were meant to supersede.

Thus Sraffa's work led him to argue in 1925 and 1926 that partial equilibrium analysis only applied to constant costs and that to argue otherwise would be inconsistent with the method used (though not necessarily with the 'real world' facts which he also discussed). This is a logical and methodological criticism, that is to say, a search for the set of conditions which allow the method logically to be applied. Sraffa starts by showing that the 'laws' of returns historically belonged in different parts of the discipline: diminishing returns in the theory of distribution (rent) rather than in the discussions of relative values, increasing returns in the discussion of 'general economic progress' rather than in a discussion of 'increase[s] in the scale of production' (1926, p. 537). To combine them together in one theoretical whole was both contradictory and restrictive. This was especially true of increasing returns, for to be consistent with competitive theory, the division of labour had to be limited to the case of 'independent subsidiary factories coming into existence as the production of an industry [increased]' (1926, p. 537). Internal economies associated with the growth in the size of an individual firm had to be 'entirely abandoned [because they were] incompatible with competitive conditions ... ' (1926, pp. 537–538). 'External economies' were therefore more and more emphasised.

The fixed factor aspect of diminishing returns meant that the more broadly we defined an industry, the more likely it was that diminishing returns (arising from using one factor) would arise. By contrast, the more homogeneous we make the commodity which the industry is to produce, (for example, we move from agriculture to fruit) 'the greater will be the probability that the forces which make for increasing returns will predominate' (1926, p. 538). Sraffa likens these effects to the effects of time, in particular the time allowed for adjustments to occur and the consequent impact of this on returns.

It is, however, the independence assumption (of demand and supply schedules in relation to small variations) which is most at risk. For, as Sraffa says,

> It is primarily in [the] ... category that ... when a variation in the quantity produced by [an] industry ... sets up a force which acts directly, not merely upon its own costs, but also on the costs of other industries [so that] the conditions of the 'particular equilibrium' which it was intended to isolate are upset ... that the applications of the laws of returns fall, in the great majority of cases [1926, p. 539].

As far as diminishing returns are concerned, we are left with 'the study of that minute class of commodities in the production of which the whole of a factor of production is employed' (1926, p. 539), while for increasing returns, we may consider only those economies which are external to the firm but internal to the industry, 'precisely the class which is most seldom to be met with [in practice]' (1926, p. 540).

So we have Sraffa's conclusion (1926, pp. 540-541) that:

> the supply schedule with variable costs cannot claim to be a

> general conception applicable to normal markets ... In normal cases the cost of production of commodities produced competitively — as we are not entitled to take into consideration the causes which may make it rise or fall — must be regarded as constant in respect of small variations in the quantity produced.

Hence the discarded cost-of-production theory of value returns 'as a simple way of approaching the problem of competitive value ... [It] is as important as it is useful: it emphasises the fundamental factor ... the predominant influence of the cost of production' (1926, p. 541). It also makes it possible to bring in other factors in more detailed analyses of the exchange values of particular commodities because 'it does not conceal from us the fact that we cannot find the elements required for this purpose *within the limits of its assumptions*' (1926, p. 541, emphasis added).

In the 1926 article, Sraffa turned his back on general equilibrium — the conditions of simultaneous equilibrium in a number of industries — 'while keeping to the path of free competition', because he felt it did not offer an accessible way out for *theory*. Instead, he spawned the imperfect competition, monopolistic competition 'revolutions' when he sketched a logically watertight theory which served to illuminate the 'real world' facts of the time: competitive structures which were associated with differentiated products and unutilised opportunities for lower costs with higher rates of output (unutilised because of insufficient demand at a profitable price).

While this approach was enthusiastically taken up, at least for a time, by the profession (Chicago always excepted), Sraffa himself had changed tack by 1930 to develop a coherent account of the surplus approach of the classical political economists — the contention that the surplus of commodities over those necessary for their reproduction is the core concept of economic theory around which theories of value, distribution, production, employment and growth may, and should, be set. In Sraffa's view this approach reached its highest form in Marx's work, only to be superseded in mainstream economics by the rise to dominance of the supply and demand theories. By stressing the production interdependencies of the economy as a whole (commodities produced by means of commodities), Sraffa set out a system which gave coherence to the surplus concept, allowed the analysis of the effect of different values of a distributive variable on prices to be examined and, at the same time, provided a critique of the marginal theories in so far as they were directed to answering classical questions about the origin and size of the rate of profits. The development of these ideas occupied many years. They were published in 1960 as *Production of Commodities by Means of Commodities*.

From 1930 on Sraffa also worked on his magnificent 11-volume edition (1951–73) of the works and correspondence of David Ricardo, in later years collaborating with Maurice Dobb, who did not share Sraffa's extreme inhibitions against writing for publication. It is one of the finest examples of sustained and meticulous scholarship in the discipline. The arguments of the introduction to volume 1, published in 1951, are important complements to those of Sraffa's 1960 book. In attempting this sustained research programme of both criticism and revival Sraffa may have had in mind Gramsci's injunction to attack at its logical core the very best expression of a rival philosophical system (see below, p. 62).

III

The first major point to make about Joan Robinson is that for good or ill she was much influenced by Marshall and by his methods, his principal preoccupations and by his acute insights. (She is on record as saying that 'the more I learn about economics the more I admire Marshall's intellect and the less I like his character' (1973a (1953), p. 259). That she understood profoundly and very early on his system of thought in the *Principles* is evident from the delightful essay, 'Beauty and the beast', which was written jointly with her great friend Dorothea Morison, afterwards Mrs R.B. Braithwaite, while she was still an undergraduate. It concludes: 'With this happy union of producer's and consumer's surplus they then lived happily ever after, constantly keeping in mind their higher ideals and maximizing their satisfaction by equalising the marginal utility of each object of expenditure' *(Collected Economic Papers*, vol. 1, 1978 (1951), p.233). Of the essay she says: '[It] owes nothing to Keynes, but everything to Marshall' (p. ix).

Much of her early technical work was explicitly Marshallian static in method. This is obvious in *The Economics of Imperfect Competition* and is the fundamental reason why she was eventually to repudiate much of the analysis. It depended upon the 'shameless fudge' that implicitly assumed that equilibrium points could remain stable while economic agents (as we would say now) actively searched for them. The same method lies behind her classic paper on 'The foreign exchanges', (1947 (1937)), which reads as though the author, having drawn up the arguments in terms of supply and demand curves and their movements, had then translated the findings into English. (Joan Robinson denied though that this was how it was written.) The lasting impact that Marshall had on her thinking was not only through the forces of supply and demand as presented in the statical methods but also through his discussion of the meaning of equilibrium and the basic inconsistency in his own system between his vision of an accumulating economy moving forward through time, on the one hand and the static equilibrium method on the other. Joan Robinson for many years thought that Marshall admitted this himself but hid it away in Appendix H. There, the irreversibility of the long-period supply curve is revealed even though in the text, in his central discussion of long-period normal prices (what Kahn (1929, p.1) has described as 'the real business of the *Principles*), long-period supply and demand curves are integral parts of the analysis.

In writing *The Economics of Imperfect Competition*, Joan Robinson developed her ideas from Sraffa's 'pregnant suggestion' that each firm was its own little monopolist in a nevertheless competitive environment; but she virtually ignored the message of his argument that it was, except for some minor, empirically unimportant, exceptions, inadmissible in competitive theory to assume that supply and demand curves were independent of each other. As Sraffa said in the 1930 symposium on 'Increasing returns and the representative firm', '[Marshall's] theory cannot be interpreted in a way which makes it logically self-consistent and at the same time, reconciles it with the facts it sets out to explain [so that] Marshall's theory ... should be discarded' (1930, p. 93).

The significance of this general criticism, that it may be inadmissible in general to draw a schedule because any actual movement along it may alter its position (and those of other schedules), was to have its full impact on Joan Robinson after World War II when it became the basis of the central criticism she was to make of what she considered to be the method of orthodox economic theory. In retrospect she was to argue that Marshall, too, had known this all along, that he had confined his formal statements to equilibrium points and had considered only notional changes around them. He had also stressed the importance of equilibrium positions being stable ones — otherwise they would not be of any interest in explaining, through the medium of supply and demand curves, the outcome of sustained and dominant, or persistent, forces.

Joan Robinson herself was to make a unique contribution here, when finally she departed radically from both the Marshallian and the neoclassical equilibrium tradition whereby a problem was always framed so as to discuss first existence and uniqueness and then local and global stability. She was to say, in effect, that these were distinctions or dichotomies without content. If a market or an economy were in equilibrium, no question of stability arose — it was as if expectations always were realised. If either were not in equilibrium, then the question of existence did not arise, because the market or the economy evolved under the influence of past and present happenings and expectations of the future, reacting to any inconsistencies now present but with no presupposition that they would seek out positions where, once again, they were absent. Hence we have her statements:

> The short period is here and now, with concrete stocks of the means of production in existence. Incompatibilities in the situation ... will determine what happens next. Long-period equilibrium is not at some date in the future; it is an imaginary state of affairs in which there are no incompatibilities in the existing situation, here and now [1965b (1962), p. 101].[3]

In the course of her life she had another 180° change of viewpoint over a second aspect of methodology.[4] Very early on, she set out her youthful views on method in an essay published in 1932, 'Economics is a serious subject'. There she argued that 'the subject matter of economics is neither more nor less than its own technique' (p.4). Joan Robinson then went on to distinguish between manageable sets of assumptions and realistic sets, adding that '[g]enerally speaking, the optimistic, English, economist will choose the manageable set and the pessimistic, methodological, Continental, economist will choose the realistic set' (pp. 6–7) and firmly allied herself with the optimists. (The pessimist was Piero Sraffa!) By the end of her life, though, she was to adopt the Continental economist's approach (and also, alas, his pessimism) and to scrap any faith that she may ever have had in 'complete theories'. (It has sometimes been said that Joan Robinson did not have the influence she should have had because she did not provide an alternative 'complete theory' to replace that of the neoclassicals. She herself considered that 'any other "complete theory" would be only another box of tricks', adding that 'we need ... a different habit of mind — to eschew fudging, to respect facts and to admit ignorance of what we do not know' (*Collected Economic Papers*, vol. V, 1979, p.119).

As we have argued, Sraffa's aim in his 1925 and 1926 papers was to show the logical incoherence of Marshall's method and its applications, i.e. that the occasions when it was legitimate to apply it, because the supply and demand curves could be taken as independent of one another, were a very small part indeed of the real world. These arguments constituted the main thrust of the two papers, but in the 1926 paper, following his masterly succinct summary of the argument of the 1925 paper, he added the section about monopoly which spawned the imperfect competition revolution. As we have argued, he himself did not follow this up but went in another direction (which was also mentioned in the 1926 paper, see Sraffa 1926, p.541): that of examining the interrelatedness of production and the relationship of this to the theory of value and distribution, the revival of the surplus approach which reached its fullest statement in *Production of Commodities*.

Theorising at this level of abstraction may not have been of much interest to Keynes, while Joan Robinson was probably not aware of the early drafts (which Sraffa had shown to Keynes in 1928, see Sraffa 1960, p. vi) when she was writing her first big book in the late 1920s and early 1930s. In addition to Sraffa's influence, Joan Robinson mentions the overriding importance of Shove's work, principally in his lectures, and, of course, of Kahn's guiding hand on virtually every page. Indeed, Keynes was to say in his report on the book to Harold Macmillan in 1932 (1983, p. 867) that he had

> a great deal of confidence that it [was] reasonably free from minor slips and errors and fallacies because it had been very elaborately and carefully criticised by R.F. Kahn. [He] is the most careful and accurate of all the younger economists, and mistakes do not easily get past him ... Knowing the part he has played ... [Keynes had] much greater confidence in its being free from the blunders which so very easily creep into a treatment of this kind.

Keynes himself thought 'that the book will be for a little while to come an essential one for any serious student of the modern theory of value' (p. 867). When writing this, Keynes did not know of Chamberlin's parallel work (Chamberlin 1933), which probably was to prove more fruitful than Joan Robinson's work and which was not influenced, at least to the same degree, by Sraffa's work.[5]

However, Keynes did know of Richard Kahn's Fellowship Dissertation for King's, *The Economics of the Short Period*, which Kahn submitted to the electors at the end of 1929, and so did Joan Robinson and Piero Sraffa. In a sense it provided the empirical back up from the experience of the United Kingdom textile industry in the 1920s as well as some of the theory which Joan Robinson was to exposit and bring to fruition in *The Economics of Imperfect Competition*. Marshallian theory, especially in its Pigouvian form, predicted that, in a slump, only those firms that could cover their short-run variable costs would be found producing. But, in fact, in industries which had experienced a sustained decline in demand, e.g. the textile industry, most firms were still to be found operating, admitedly well below normal levels of capacity, and at prices which exceeded their average variable costs. Joan Robinson and her colleagues exploited the concept of the marginal revenue curve together with Sraffa's notion of a downward sloping demand curve for the competitive firm to explain this phenomenon. The profit-maximising prices and outputs are determined by the intersections of their marginal revenues and marginal cost curves. The analysis illuminates the real world facts (alluded to by Sraffa) that businessmen felt that it was demand conditions rather than rising costs which limited their sales and that firms could make profits even with plants running well below capacity.

In any event Joan Robinson had already become excited about the critique of the *Treatise* and the emerging propositions of the *General Theory*. She took an active part not only in writing papers which were progress reports on the way, for example 'The theory of money and the analysis of output', (1978 (1933)), but also in commenting on drafts of the *General Theory* as Keynes prepared them and in drafting even before its publication her own 'told to the children' version which was to become *Introduction to the Theory of Employment* (1937). Already in 1933 Joan Robinson had a very clear perception that the theory of money, the theory of demand

and supply of output (as a whole) and the theory of prices should be intertwined. (She was not alone, of course; others had been there before, for example D.H. Robertson and R.G. Hawtrey.) She gives a very clear description of how a decline in output (in the *Treatise* framework) will bring about the equality of saving with a (given) level of investment, commenting that Keynes had missed the profound significance of this result, throwing

> it out in the most casual way without pausing to remark that he [had] proved that output may be in equilibrium at any number of different levels ... that while there is a natural tendency towards equilibrium between savings and investment ... there is no natural tendency towards full employment of the factors of production ... [Keynes had] failed to notice [when he wrote the *Treatise*] that he had incidentally evolved a new theory of the long-period analysis of output [1978 (1933), p. 56].

As Keynes moved towards the publication of the *General Theory*, Joan Robinson was extending his analysis in two directions, her first try at a long-period theory of effective demand (1947 (1936)) and her work on the international aspects of Keynes's theory (for example, Part III, 1947 (1937)). Her work on the long-period theory of employment was still Marshallian in method and neoclassical in regard to the treatment of the distribution of income, though, of course, it took into account Keynes's theory of output as a whole and the monetary nature of the rate of interest. She took as given the level of the rate of interest and asked the analytical question whether, when the stock of capital goods has adjusted optimally to this rate of interest so that we have a stationary state (a Marshallian long-period position) in which net investment is zero, we would find associated with that stock a fully employed labour force. The concept of the elasticity of substitution plays a key role in the determination of the overall distribution of income both in the long-period position and in the discussion of the transition to it.[6] (Keynes's insight was to ask whether the long-period level of income which allowed net saving to be zero also implied long-period unemployment.) The paper also contains an extension to the long period of the proposition established in the short-period analysis of the *General Theory*: that a rise in the desire to save may in fact decrease output and employment.

As we mentioned earlier, Sraffa was increasingly distancing

himself from these particular discussions, though it is clear from his correspondence with Joan Robinson over the 1930s that he was trying to persuade her and others close to Keynes of the 'emptiness' of the marginal productivity theory of value and distribution. Indeed, he argued that there was quite a theological flavour to the concepts and arguments of the subjective theory of value. For example, there is a letter in October 1936 in which he explicitly refers to the incoherence of the concept of a quantity of capital (measured in a unit which is independent of distribution and prices) relative to the concepts of land and labour. He suggests that if Joan Robinson were to ask her gardener what a quantity of capital was, he would think her dotty, though he would have no trouble in understanding what quantities of land and labour were. It seems reasonable to suppose that the force of these arguments impressed itself upon her when she began to think about the problems of growth and accumulation in the post-war period. Sraffa himself returned to this theme, that it was impossible to find a unit in which to measure capital that was independent of distribution and prices, in his published work in the post-war period, for example, at several places in his 1960 book and in his 1962 reply to Harrod. Thus: 'One can only wonder what is the good of a quantity of capital or a period of production which, since it depends on the rate of interest, cannot be used for its traditional purpose, which is to determine the rate of interest' (1962, p. 479).

As I have argued elsewhere, see Harcourt (1979, 1982, 1984b), the quantum jump in Joan Robinson's thinking came when she started seriously to study Marx and Marxism. It is interesting to compare her early views, as expressed in her review, 'Some reflections on Marxist economics', (1936b (1947)), of John Strachey's *The Nature of Capitalist Crisis* (1935), where she appears to argue that Marx was a classical economist because he accepted Say's law, with her later much more incisive and sympathetic views (except in regard to the labour theory of value) in, for example, her 1942 *Essay on Marxian Economics*[7] and her 1951 introduction to the English edition of Rosa Luxemburg's *Accumulation of Capital* (which is reprinted in *Collected Economic Papers*, vol. II, 1975 (1960)). Sraffa, of course, had always 'known' his Marx from his early student days and saw in Marx's work the fulfilment of the surplus approach, the origins of which were to be found in the Physiocrats and Adam Smith and Ricardo. Reading Marx's work, writing her book on him and her friendship with Kalecki which dates from the mid-1930s, radically changed Joan Robinson's perspective. In particular, the reproduction schemes from which Kalecki started his discussion of the theory of effective demand, the nature of the trade cycle and the theory of distribution were increasingly to become Joan Robinson's mode of thought so that when she started to write on capital and growth theory, it was the natural framework to use. It is also significant that in her introduction to Rosa Luxemburg's book, she poses as the key question, 'Where does the demand come from which keeps the accumulation going?' (*Collected Economic Papers*, vol. II, 1975, (1960), p.65).[8]

Harrod's work on dynamics was also another major influence although she was able to show him that he exemplified that attractive English vice of unnecessary originality, that his theory was essentially to be found in volume II of *Capital* (*Collected Economic Papers*, vol, IV, 1973 (1953), p.263). Harrod himself thought he was doing something much more fundamental for economic theory than Keynes had, because he was providing the foundations of dynamic analysis, i.e. rediscovering volume II in which it is shown that once a capitalist economy 'slips off [an equilibrium line of development] it will never get back between now and doomsday', (see Joan Robinson *Collected Economic Papers*, vol. IV, 1973 (1953), p.263).

IV

The Accumulation of Capital (1956) is Joan Robinson's *magnum opus*. She published it when she was the same age as Keynes had been when he published the *General Theory* and she meant it to do for the long-period problems of growth and distribution what he had done for the short-period problems of the theory of effective demand. As it was to do with the long period she felt that she needed a theory of the rate of profits and that Sraffa (in his introduction to the Ricardo volumes, Sraffa with Dobb 1951) had provided a coherent theory to replace what she discerned as incoherent in Marshall, from whom she originally learnt her theory of value and distribution. There is in her papers a draft of a preface to a later edition of *The Accumulation of Capital* which explains very clearly the four main sorts of issues and questions with which she was concerned. This list also shows why it was a difficult book to grasp in its entirety. As far as I have been able to discover the preface has never been published, at least in English; it appears from internal evidence to have been written either in or after 1959.

Joan Robinson considers a model of an unregulated free enterprise economy in which firms 'within the limits set by their command of finance' determine the rate of capital accumulation, while the members of the public, constrained 'by their command of purchasing power, are free to make the rate of expenditure what they please, ... [a] model ... not ... unrealistic in essential respects'. The model may be used 'to analyse the chances and changes of the development of an economy as time goes by' by considering 'four distinct groups of questions':

> 1. We make comparisons of situations, each with its own past, developing into its own future, which are different in some respect (for instance the rate of accumulation going on in each) in order to see what the postulated difference entails.
> 2. We trace the path which a single economy follows when the technical conditions (including their rate of change) and the propensities to consume and to invest are constant through time.
> 3. We trace the consequences of a change in any of these conditions for the future development of the economy.
> 4. We examine the short period reaction of the economy to unexpected events.

The first group of questions is more naturally handled in terms of comparisons of steady states (including stationary states). The conditions for steady states to be achieved are set out, but there is no implication that the unregulated behaviour of the decision makers will in fact ever bring them about. When discussing the choice of techniques, the relationship between the value of capital and physical capital in the economy as a whole becomes relevant and 'takes up several chapters (Book II, Section II) and is difficult out of all proportion to its importance'.

The second set of questions concerns what happens when one of the conditions for steady growth (other than technical conditions and the consumption propensities) is not satisfied. The third set relates to the path which the economy will follow when, having been in a steady state, a basic change, for example, 'an increase in monopoly which causes profit margins to increase', occurs. The fourth set concerns the reactions of the inducement to invest to current events in an uncertain world and relates to the possibility of oscillation in the transition from one state of affairs to another or even to the generation of a trade cycle by 'mere uncertainty' without any change in basic conditions. In principle, says Joan Robinson, 'this type of analysis enables us to deal with all the possible vicissitudes of a developing economy, and prepares the way for discussions of public policy'.

The central analytical structure of the book eventually came to be associated with her famous banana diagram of the two-sided relationship that she discerned between profitability and accumulation. On the one hand, the rate of accumulation of capital goods is a major determinant of actual profitability. (Here Kalecki's influence many be discerned, workers spending what they earn and capitalists receiving what they spend.) On the other hand, the planned rate of accumulation is itself a function of expected profitability, taking as given the conditions relating to the cost and availability of finance, including retained profits and the state of long-term expectations. Here we may discern Keynes's influence and Joan Robinson explicitly acknowledged it at this point by referring to this particular relationship as the 'animal spirits' function, a reference to the passage on p.161 of the *General Theory*:

> Most, probably, of our decisions to do something positive, the full consequences of which will be drawn out over many days to come, can only be taken as a result of animal spirits — of a spontaneous urge to action rather than inaction, and not as the outcome of a weighted average of quantitative benefits multiplied by quantitative probabilities.

If we assume there to be a link between achieved profitability and expected probability (let us make it one-to-one for expositional purposes, i.e. what has happened is expected to happen again), we obtain the following relationships for given states of long-term expectations (see Figure 3.1): $r = r\ (g)$ is the first relationship, where r is the realised rate of profits and g is the realised rate of accumulation. (The simplest form of this relationship is $r = g/s_c$, where s_c is the saving propensity of the capitalist class, the so-called Cambridge equation for r.) $g^* = g^*\ (r^*)$ is the second relationship, where g^* is the planned rate of accumulation and r^* is expected profitability.

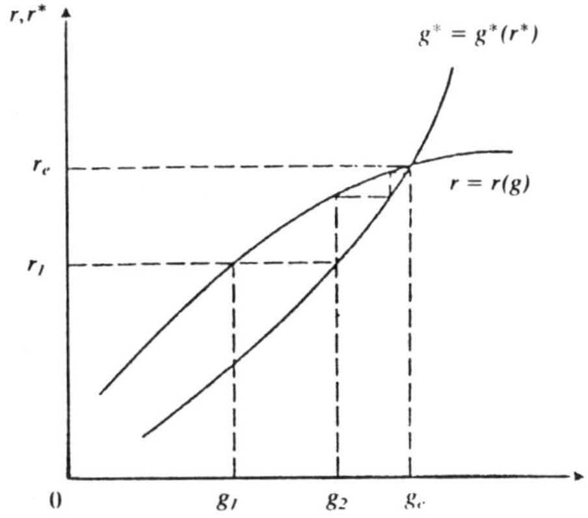

Figure 3.1

If the actual rate of accumulation were g_l at a particular point in time, realised profitability would be r_l. This in turn, implies expected profitability of r_l which induces a rate of accumulation of g_2. If the two functions are stable — one of Joan Robinson's major points is that there is little reason to suppose that they should be — and provided that the $g^* = g^* (r^*)$ relationship is fairly inelastic, an iterative process takes the economy to the intersection of the two schedules, g_e, r_e. This is a sort of equilibrium in the sense that the accumulation that was induced by certain expectations in fact fulfils them so that in the absence of changes in underlying conditions, the economy will tend to stay accumulating at this rate. But it is a very limited result, for it makes only the capitalists happy — there is nothing to guarantee that this rate of accumulation will fully employ the labour force nor are there any mechanisms in the model to cause the economy to seek out such a rate of growth or even to ensure that the economy stays at r_e, g_e position. The mere passage of time and bunching of replacements or the arrival of innovations can redefine the underlying functions.

We noted earlier why the list showed that *The Accumulation of Capital* was a difficult book to grasp in its entirety. Tom Asimakopulos (in a letter of 14 January 1985) has suggested to me that the list also provides a clue as to why it 'failed' ... despite the many excellent things in it: that Joan Robinson

> never discussed the various strands of her analysis, their interrelationships and their compatibility, or lack of it, with her 'Keynes' view of the world. Her later critical essays provide some insight on how she would handle these questions but she never published anything directly on them.

V

Parallel with Joan Robinson's developments and discussion of these issues was her attack on the neoclassical theory of value and distribution, expressed principally in the aggregate production function version of, for example, J.B. Clark and Hicks's *Theory of Wages*. This was extended into her critique of neoclassical growth models when Solow, Swan, Samuelson and Meade responded to the questions opened up by Harrod (and Domar) by trying purposefully[9] to provide neoclassical answers. While Joan Robinson's critique started within the context of the overall choice of technique within a growth model, it soon developed into both a methodological critique and a discussion of the *meaning* of capital within the supply and demand frameworks (of Marshall, Walras and Fisher) and within a model of a capitalist economy generally. Perhaps the most comprehensive statement of her ultimate position (except in regard to Sraffa's model, for which we must go to 'Spring cleaning' (1985 (1980)) is her paper in the *Revue d'Economie Politique* symposium of 1977. (The English translation is essay 5 in *Collected Economic Papers*, vol. V, 1979.) In the early days of the debate, it was the former issues which dominated and this emphasis was reinforced by the publication of *Production of Commodities* in 1960. The chapters on reduction to dated labour, and fixed capital, and Part III — Sraffa's discussion of capital reversing and reswitching — reinforced and put into focus the results that had come out of Joan Robinson's work and comments upon it, especially the remarkable comment in 1953-54 by David Champernowne.[10] Thus, the implications of marginal productivity theory in its simplest form — that there were inverse relationships between the rate of profits and 'capital' per person, the 'capital'–

output ratio, and sustainable levels of consumption per person, implications which were rigorously established in models with one all-purpose commodity — were shown not to be robust once the inescapable fact of life that 'capital' in one of its forms is durable hard objects was admitted into the analysis. Especially damaging was thought to be the destruction of the inevitability of a well-behaved downward sloping demand curve for 'capital', a result that was implicit in the capital-reversing and reswitching propositions.

For some little time these arguments were thought to be conclusive, especially when Samuelson accepted them in his 'summing-up' paper in the 1966 *Quarterly Journal of Economics* symposium, following the failure of his pupil Levhari to refute them in 1965. But while Joan Robinson initially welcomed these results she had decided by the late 1960s that they were a side issue and that her methodological critique relating to changes versus differences was the central issue. (I know because the major complaint that she made about the first draft of my 1972 book which I sent to her in about May 1970 was that I had not emphasised the methodological critique sufficiently.) Her most explicit personal statement of this view is to be found in 'The unimportance of reswitching' (1979b (1975)). This emphasis was to separate her for the rest of her life from her former allies, probably Piero Sraffa himself and, more actively, John Eatwell, Murray Milgate and Pierangelo Garegnani. Indeed, it is necessary to separate her attitude to Sraffa from her attitude to the other three scholars, partly because her discussions with them concerned Keynesian questions — whether Keynes himself had provided a short-period or long-period analysis and, if he had not, or had not done it adequately, what form would the long-period theory of effective demand take?

In 'Spring cleaning' Joan Robinson put Sraffa's contributions into focus, in so far as they bore on her particular interests, making a distinction between the nature of the model which underlay the first two parts of the book, on the one hand and that which underlay the third part on the other. In the first two, we enter the world just as it is at the moment with the stocks of means of production already established because of past decisions in the light of past expectations. We are given the value of one distributive variable (Joan Robinson makes it the share of wages in value-added) and then find the corresponding values of the prices of production and the other distributive variable, here the rate of profits. Because we assume a uniform rate of profits we have prices of production. This is not a description of 'reality', or a theory of market prices, but an analytical construction. In Sraffa's system, certainly as used by the Sraffians, though not in anything Sraffa himself wrote,[11] the prices of production are centres of gravitation. Presumably, therefore, they have some explanatory power for the patterns of actual market prices — but this is not so in Joan Robinson's interpretation. She has, though, abandoned her earlier interpretation whereby the means of production were such that, in effect, a stationary state with all things in their correct proportions was established. Now, she says, this may or may not be; we take the world as we find it and do our thought experiments.

When we get to Part III, we change our perspective, as Sraffa hints in his preface: 'No changes in output and (at any rate in parts I and II) no changes in the proportions in which different means of production are used by an industry are considered' (p. v). We now look at a producer who is to make a choice between two (or more) possible ways of producing a commodity. Sraffa takes great pains to allow such a comparison logically to be made. Joan Robinson says that it cannot be done:

> [We] can imagine a variety of techniques for producing a single flow output set up in a 'book of blueprints' but we cannot imagine switching from one to another at an instant of time. A switch would require availability of the appropriate stocks of inputs already in existence. Moreover, differences in techniques are introduced successively through time as research and development goes on responding to historical changes not merely to shifts in the rate of profit.

She adds: 'To put the point in methodological terms, it is not correct to draw two or more wage-profit curves in the same axes, for the *y* axis represents the flow of net output in only one particular technique' (1985 (1980), p. 164).

There is, moreover, a further problem of measurement, even in terms of Sraffa's own construction of a Standard commodity. Each system has its own Standard commodity and it is not therefore possible to find a consistent measure with which to make comparisons between the systems. Ricardo's search for an invariant standard of value was really a search for a will o' the wisp. Thus,

Joan Robinson argues that Sraffa's procedure is an illegitimate comparison in that it cannot illuminate processes actually going on in historical time. Such a procedure *is* allowed a role in doctrinal debates whereby the marginal productivity theory of distribution is attacked and the concepts of the marginal product of capital and the demand curve for capital are argued to be vacuous. At this point, she says, we leave Sraffa and take up again with Keynes — and Kalecki (see Bhaduri and Joan Robinson 1980).

Finally, in her debates with Garegnani, and with Eatwell and Milgate, Joan Robinson used her views on the inadmissibility of long-period comparisons for describing processes, which she developed in her critique of neoclassical theory,[12] to criticise the central stress by these authors on the notion of centres of gravitation or long-period positions. Here, her final departure from Marshall's definition of the long period which we noted above is relevant, for it was this that made her reject in a theory of accumulation and distribution — a process in historical time — any use of the notion of a centre of gravitation. In effect, she was moving close to rejecting the usefulness of the issues discussed under the first two, possibly the first three, headings in the unpublished preface to *The Accumulation of Capital* and to concentrating entirely on the fourth issue, as it was developed, for example, in Kalecki's theories of cyclical growth.[13] It was in *that* form, she argued, that we were to find the essential messages of Keynes — and of Marx. This was a brave, if depressing and nearly nihilistic conclusion to which to come. As ever, as we said before, she may have been too hard on herself.

VI

Sraffa, as we have argued, saw his positive contribution as having sorted out some unfinished or incoherent problems within the whole corpus of Marx's theory of the laws of motion of capitalism, by reviving the surplus approach in a rigorous manner. The late Ronald Meek was the first of the reviewers of *Production of Commodities* to discern in the book a rehabilitation, or revival, of classical economics (including, in this description, Marx's contributions). In his perceptive review article, 'Mr Sraffa's rehabilitation of classical economics', first published in 1961 and reprinted in Meek (1967), he showed, especially in the last section, that the structure of Sraffa's system was such as to provide a rigorous formal content for Marx's insight that the origin of profit was the surplus labour extracted in the sphere of production from the wage-earning class by the capitalist class. This showed itself as surplus value — here the form which Marx gave to the labour theory of value is relevant — which was reflected in the sphere of distribution and exchange as the component of average profits in the prices of production. The prices of production themselves, and their divergence from the Marxian labour values of the sphere of production, could be predicted from the knowledge of these labour values and two other embodied labour amounts, those associated with the net product and means of production of Sraffa's Standard system, which when expressed as a ratio, constituted the maximum rate of profits of the economic system (*R*). According to Meek, Marx himself had used his own construction of an average industry — one which showed in its organic composition of capital the characteristics of the economy as a whole — in order to make the same point as Sraffa in his (Marx's) solution of the transformation problem (see Meek 1967, pp. 175–178). The Standard commodity is a composite commodity in which each individual commodity appears in the same proportion in its output as it does in the inputs or means of production. The Standard system is an imaginary rearrangement of the actual system such that the same total amount of labour is 'employed' but the levels of activity of the individual industries are so rearranged as to make the net product have commodities in it in Standard commodity proportions; the means of production, of course, also exhibit the same proportions.

Some commentators have interpreted these concepts and the analysis in which they are used as Sraffa's solution to Ricardo's unsolved problem, the search for an invariable standard of value. This is too limited an interpretation. In so far as Sraffa's contribution bears on Ricardo's problem — it will be remembered that Ricardo wanted to find such a unit because he wanted to be able to say rigorous things about the distribution of the surplus of heterogeneous commodities between classes both when distribution changed and technical advances occurred — Sraffa shows conclusively that Ricardo was searching for a will o' the wisp. While it is true, at least in a circulating commodity model without joint production, that a Standard commodity which is invariant to changes in distribution is always waiting to be found at a particular point of time, any changes in the level of any of the basic industries (unless they exhibit constant returns to scale), or any technical advance in the basic industries which alters the amounts of the means of production and/or labour needed to produce any basic commodity, immediately implies that there is another, completely different, Standard commodity involved. It follows that while the Standard commodity (under the assumptions stated) will serve to solve one aspect of Ricardo's problem — the impact of changes in distribution on the measurement of the surplus (the exact form of this relationship must be interpreted very carefully) — it does not solve the other aspect associated with changes in activity and with technical advances. Even with the first aspect, we must note that what is revealed, having previously been hidden, is an inverse relationship between the *rate* of profits and the wage (which in terms of the Standard commodity is a simple linear relationship), but not necessarily an inverse relationship between the *shares* of profits and wages (see Sraffa 1960, p. 23).

However, the principal purpose of the Standard commodity and the Standard system, together with the associated relationship, $r = R(1-w)$ (where r = rate of profits, R = maximum rate of profits and w = wage measured in terms of the Standard commodity and as a share of the Standard national income), is rigorously to reveal what Ricardo, and later Marx, were striving for in their theory of the origin of profits. As Meek and Christopher Gregory have shown, the line which runs from Ricardo to Marx to Sraffa may be shown schematically as follows:[14]

$$r = \frac{\text{Corn as output} - \text{corn as capital (advances of necessaries to labour)}}{\text{Corn as capital (advances of necessaries to labour)}} \quad \text{(Ricardo of the } \textit{Essay}\text{)} \quad (1)$$

$$1 + r = \frac{\text{Total labour}}{\text{Labour in necessaries}} \quad \text{(Ricardo of the } \textit{Principles}\text{)} \quad (2)$$

In Marx's terms, this becomes:

$$1 + r = \frac{s + v}{v} \tag{3}$$

and for Marx himself,

$$r = \frac{(s + v) - v}{v + c} = \frac{s + v}{c} \cdot \frac{c}{c + v} \cdot \frac{s}{s + v}$$

$$= R.k\left\{1 - \frac{v}{s + v}\right\} \tag{4}$$

where

$\frac{s + v}{c}$ is the maximum rate of profits, R

$\frac{c}{c + v}$ is the organic composition of capital, k

s = surplus value
v = variable capital
c = constant capital

all measured in terms of labour time.

Because the wage is paid out of the surplus in Sraffa's formulation, we have

$$r = \frac{s}{c} = \frac{s + v}{c}\left\{1 - \frac{v}{s + v}\right\} \tag{5}$$

(Note that there is now no longer a place for the organic composition of capital in this formulation.)

Finally, in Sraffa's analysis, (5) becomes

$$r = R(1 - w) \tag{6}$$

rigorously measured in terms of the Standard commodity, as Meek showed long ago.

VII

As far as Sraffa's prelude to a critique was concerned, it does seem fair to say that he helped to undermine the central thrust of the supply and demand theories, in so far as they were directed towards answering classical questions about the origin and size of the rate of profits, by showing some of their principal messages to be either incoherent or illogical. This is especially so concerning a unit in which to measure 'capital', the lack of coherence in the concept of 'its' marginal product, and the inability to privide plausible conditions for the construction of a well-behaved demand curve for 'capital'. The debates themselves still continue, now placed more securely within the context of general equilibrium analysis (see, for example, Hahn's 1982 paper on 'The neo-Ricardians'). But, whatever the outcome of this particular line of thought, the following passage from Gramsci on 'The intellectuals', which was read at the memorial service for Piero Sraffa in November 1983, will stand as a valid account of the ideals and objectives of these two great twentieth-century political economists.

> In a political and military struggle it can be correct tactics to break through at the points of least resistance in order to be able to assault the strongest point with maximum forces that have been precisely made available by the elimination of the weaker auxiliaries... On the ideological front, however, the degree of the auxiliaries and the minor hangers-on is of all but negligible importance. Here it is necessary to engage battle with the most eminent of one's adversaries. Otherwise, one confuses newspapers with books, and petty polemic with scientific work. The lesser figures must be abandoned to the infinite casebook of newspaper polemic.
>
> A new science proves its efficacy and vitality when it demonstrates that it is capable of confronting the great champions of the tendencies opposed to it and when it either resolves by its own means the vital questions which they have posed or demonstrates, in peremptory fashion, that these questions are false problems.
>
> It is true that an historical epoch and a given society are characterised rather by the average run of intellectuals, and therefore by the more mediocre. But widespread, mass ideology must be distinguished from the scientific works and the great philosophical syntheses which are its real corner-stones. It is the latter which must be overcome, either

negatively, by demonstrating that they are without foundation, or positively, by opposing to them philosophical syntheses of greater importance and significance.

Quaderni del carcere

Notes

1. 'Don Patinkin disputes the importance commonly attributed to [the 'circus'] in assisting Keynes to write the *General Theory. In so far as he relies on documents*, he is fully entitled to make his case' (Kahn 1984, p. 105, emphasis added).
2. We know so far of 18 letters from Sraffa to Joan Robinson, spanning the period from 1931 to 1951, in Joan Robinson's papers in the King's library. Whether Joan Robinson's corresponding letters are in Sraffa's papers is not yet known. In a few cases, Sraffa returned Joan Robinson's letters so that she could follow his detailed comments on her arguments.
3. See, also, Gram and Walsh (1983, p. 531) where they conclude that 'standard stability arguments find no place in Robinson's cannon'.
4. This is not criticism but praise. Her favourite story about Keynes is that when someone remonstrated with him for being inconsistent, he responded, 'When someone persuades me that I am wrong, I change my mind. What do you do?'
5. Chamberlin himself says (p. 5, note 4) that while 'there are striking parallels (in Sraffa's 1926 article) with some of the ideas presented in [Chamberlin 1933, yet] [a]t the time when Professor Sraffa's article appeared, the present study, submitted as a doctor's thesis at Harvard University, April, 1927 was virtually completed'.
6. While Joan Robinson herself was never to return to this issue in this particular form, there has recently been renewed interest in the paper itself: see Eatwell (1983), Kregel (1983) and O'Shaughnessy (1984).
7. Here is Keynes's reaction (20 August 1942) to her 1942 *Essay* ... He found it 'most fascinating, — as well written as anything you have done. This is in spite of the fact that there is something intrinsically boring in an attempt to make sense of what is in fact not sense.' Keynes was left with the feeling ... that [Marx] had a penetrating and original flair but was a very poor thinker indeed, — and his failure to publish the later volumes probably meant that he was not unaware of this himself. I am indebted to Robert Skidelsky for bringing this letter to my attention.
8. Shove pointed out in his review article (1944, pp. 47–48) of her 1942 book that she had misunderstood Marx's analysis with regard to Say's law and its refutation, that 'it is doubtful whether Marx anticipated modern ideas about the nature and significance of "effective demand" to the extent which her account of his theory of crises would suggest'.

9. It is perhaps, too, often forgotten, not least by his critics, that Solow (1970 (1956), p. 189) wrote: 'Everything above is the neoclassical side of the coin ... it is full employment economics — in the dual aspect of equilibrium condition and frictionless, competitive, causal system. All the difficulties and rigidities which go into modern Keynesian income analysis have been shunted aside ... not [Solow's] contention that these problems don't exist, nor that they are of no significance in the long run. (Solow's) purpose was to examine ... the tight-rope view of economic growth and to see whether more flexible assumptions about production would lead to a simple model.' Even if, as Kregel (1980) has definitively shown, Harrod did *not* assume rigidity of coefficients, Solow's way of putting the issues may be looked at as an interesting problem in its own right.
10. I do not mean to imply that Sraffa himself drew on Joan Robinson's account of capital reversing and reswitching. In all probability he had discovered them for himself, and had seen the implications of the results long before, see Sraffa (1960, p. vi) where he refers to the the 'central propositions' of *Production of Commodities* having 'taken shape in the late 1920s'. Moreover, he does not list either capital reversing or reswitching amongst either the 'particular points [which] were worked out in the 'thirties or early 'forties [or the] gaps which became apparent (while) these pages were being put together out of a mass of old notes'. Joan Robinson herself describes their respective roles in the early part of the story in the review of Ferguson (1969), see Joan Robinson (1973b(1970), p. 145).
11. Perhaps this is too strong. On page 9 of Sraffa (1960), for example, we read: 'A less one-sided description than cost of production seems therefore required. Such classical terms as "necessary price", "natural price" or "price of production" would meet the case, but value and price have been preferred as being shorter and in the present context (which contains no reference to market prices) no more ambiguous'. I am indebted to Pierangelo Garegnani for pointing out to me the significance of this passage for the present discussion.
12. Or possibly even earlier. Jan Kregel (letter of 14 January 1985) refers to 'traces of discussions (of this) with Kalecki dating from the mid-1930s'.
13. Already in 1973 she had written: 'In reality, all the interesting and important questions lie in the gap between short-period and pure long-period analysis' (1979a (1973), p. 261).
14. Christopher Gregory has a fine paper (which, alas, has never been published) in which he shows that the initial link in this chain was Quesnay. Sraffa himself provides convincing evidence of this view point in Appendix D of Sraffa (1960), 'References to the literature'; see, especially, pp. 93–94.

References

Bhaduri, Amit and Joan Robinson (1980) 'Accumulation and exploitation: an analysis in the tradition of Marx, Sraffa and Kalecki', *Cambridge Journal of Economics*, vol. 4, pp.103–115.

Chamberlin, Edward H. (1933) *The Theory of Monopolistic Competition: A Re-orientation of the Theory of Value*, Harvard University Press.

Champernowne, D.G. (1953–54) 'The production function and the theory of capital: a comment', *Review of Economic Studies*, vol. 21, no. 2, pp. 112–135.

Eatwell, J.L. (1983) 'The long-period theory of employment', *Cambridge Journal of Economics*, vol. 7, pp. 269–285.

Ferguson, C.E. (1969) *The Neoclassical Theory of Production and Distribution*, Cambridge University Press.

Garegnani, Pierangelo (1976) 'On a change in the notion of equilibrium in recent work on value and distribution', in M. Brown, K. Sato and P. Zarembka (eds), *Essays in Modern Capital Theory*, North Holland (reprinted in John Eatwell and Murray Milgate (eds), *Keynes's Economics and the Theory of Value and Distribution*, Duckworth, 1983, pp. 129–145).

Gram, Harvey and Vivian Walsh (1983) 'Joan Robinson's economics in retrospect', *Journal of Economic Literature*, vol. 21, pp. 518–550.

Hahn, F.H. (1982) 'The neo-Ricardians', *Cambridge Journal of Economics*, vol. 6, pp. 353–374.

Harcourt, G.C. (1979) 'Robinson, Joan', in David L. Sills (ed.), *International Encyclopedia of the Social Sciences, Biographical Supplement*, vol. 18, The Free Press, pp. 663–671.

Harcourt, G.C., (Prue Kerr, ed.) (1982) *The Social Science Imperialists: Selected Essays*, Routledge and Kegan Paul.

Harcourt, G.C. (1984a) 'The end of an era: Joan Robinson (1903–83) and Piero Sraffa (1898–1983)', *Journal of Post Keynesian Economics*, vol. 6, pp. 446-469.

Harcourt, G.C. (1984b) 'Harcourt on Robinson', in Henry W. Spiegel and Warren J. Samuels (eds), *Contemporary Economists in Perspective*, JAI Press, pp. 639–654.

Kahn, R.F. (1929) 'The economics of the short period', unpublished Fellowship Dissertation, King's College, Cambridge.

Kahn, R.F. (1984) *The Making of Keynes' General Theory*, Cambridge University Press.

Keynes, J.M. (1971) *A Treatise on Money*, vol. I, Macmillan for the Royal Economic Society (First published in 1930).

Keynes, J.M. (1971) *A Treatise on Money*, vol. II, Macmillan for the Royal Economic Society (First published in 1930).

Keynes, J.M. (1973) *The Collected Writings of John Maynard Keynes*, vol. XII, Macmillan for the Royal Economic Society.

Keynes, J.M. (1983) *The Collected Writings of John Maynard Keynes*,

vol. XIII, Macmillan for the Royal Economic Society.
Kregel, J.A. (1980) 'Economic dynamics and the theory of steady growth: an historical essay on Harrod's "knife-edge"', *History of Political Economy*, vol. 12, pp. 97–123.
Kregel, J.A. (1983) 'The microfoundations of the "generalisation of the *General Theory*" and "bastard Keynesianism": Keynes's theory of employment in the long and the short period', *Cambridge Journal of Economics*, vol. 7, pp. 343–361.
Levhari, D. (1965) 'A nonsubstitution theorem and switching of techniques', *Quarterly Journal of Economics*, vol. 79, pp. 98–105.
Luxemburg, Rosa (1951) *The Accumulation of Capital*, Routledge and Kegan Paul.
Meek, R.L. (1967) *Economics and Ideology and Other Essays: Studies in the Development of Economic Thought*, Chapman and Hall.
Milgate, Murray (1979) 'On the origin of the notion of "intertemporal equilibrium"', *Economica*, vol. 46, pp. 1–10.
O'Shaughnessy, T.J. (1984) 'Long-period and short-period interpretations of the principle of effective demand in a monetary economy: Keynes and Joan Robinson', mimeo, Cambridge.
Robinson, Austin (1977) 'Keynes and his Cambridge colleagues', in Don Patinkin and J. Clark Leith (eds), *Keynes, Cambridge and The General Theory*, Macmillan, pp. 25–38.
Robinson, Joan (1932) *Economics is a Serious Subject: The Apologia of an Economist to the Mathematician, the Scientist and the Plain Man*, Heffer.
Robinson, Joan (1933) *The Economics of Imperfect Competition*, Macmillan.
Robinson, Joan (1936a) 'The long-period theory of employment', *Zeitschrift für Nationalökonomie*, vol. 7, no. 1, pp. 74–93; reprinted (except for section 5) in 1947, pp. 75–100.
Robinson, Joan (1936b) 'Some reflections on Marxist economics', review of John Strachey's *The Nature of Capitalist Crisis* (1935), *Economic Journal*, vol. 46, pp. 298–302, reprinted in 1947.
Robinson, Joan (1937) *Introduction to the Theory of Employment*, Macmillan.
Robinson, Joan (1942) *An Essay on Marxian Economics*, Macmillan.
Robinson, Joan (1947) *Essays in the Theory of Employment*, Basil Blackwell (first published 1937).
Robinson, Joan (1951–79) *Collected Economic Papers*, 5 vols, Basil Blackwell.
Robinson, Joan (1956) *The Accumulation of Capital*, Macmillan.
Robinson, Joan (1965a) 'Prelude to a critique of economic theory', in Joan Robinson, *Collected Economic Papers*, vol. III, Basil Blackwell, pp. 7–14 (first published in 1961 in *Oxford Economic Papers*, vol. 13, pp. 53–58).
Robinson, Joan (1965b) Review of H.G. Johnson, *Money, Trade and*

Economic Growth (1962), in Joan Robinson, *Collected Economic Papers*, vol. III, Basil Blackwell, pp. 100–102 (first published in 1962 in *Economic Journal*, vol. 72, pp. 690–692).

Robinson, Joan (1973a) 'On re-reading Marx', in Joan Robinson, *Collected Economic Papers*, vol. IV, Basil Blackwell, pp. 247–268 (first published in 1953 by Students' Bookshops Ltd).

Robinson, Joan (1973b) 'Capital theory up-to-date', in Joan Robinson, *Collected Economic Papers*, vol. IV, Basil Blackwell, pp. 144–154 (first published in 1970 in *Canadian Journal of Economics*, vol. 3, pp. 309–317).

Robinson, Joan (1978) 'The theory of money and the analysis of output', in Joan Robinson, *Collected Economic Papers*, vol. I, Basil Blackwell (first published in 1933 in *Review of Economic Studies*, vol. 1, pp. 22–26).

Robinson, Joan (1979a) 'Ideology and analysis', in Joan Robinson, *Collected Economic Papers*, vol. V, Basil Blackwell, pp. 254–261 (first published in 1973 in *Socialismus, Geschichte und Wirtschaft, Festschrift für Eduard Marz*, Europaverlag A.G. Wien, pp. 53–60).

Robinson, Joan (1979b) 'The unimportance of reswitching', in Joan Robinson, *Collected Economic Papers*, vol. V, Basil Blackwell, pp. 26–83 (first published in 1975 in *Quarterly Journal of Economics*, vol. 89, pp. 32–39).

Robinson, Joan (1985) 'The theory of normal prices and reconstruction of economic theory', in George R. Feiwel (ed.), *Issues in Contemporary Macroeconomics and Distribution*, Macmillan, pp. 157–165 (first produced in mimeo in 1980 as 'Spring cleaning').

Robinson, Joan with Frank Wilkinson (1985) 'Ideology and logic', in Fausto Vicarelli (ed.), *Keynes's Relevance Today*, Macmillan, pp. 73–98 (first published in 1983 as 'Ideologia e logica', in Fausto Vicarelli (ed.), *Attualita di Keynes*, Editori Laterza, pp. 109–144).

Samuelson, Paul A. (1966) 'A summing up', *Quarterly Journal of Economics*, vol. 80, pp. 568–583.

Shove, G.F. (1944) 'Mrs Robinson on Marxian economics', *Economic Journal*, vol. 54, pp. 47–61.

Solow, R.M. (1970) 'A contribution to the theory of economic growth', in A.K. Sen (ed.), *Growth Economics: Selected Readings*, Penguin, pp. 161–192 (first published in Quarterly Journal of Economics, vol. 70, pp. 65–94).

Sraffa, Piero (1920) *L'inflazione monetaria in Italia durante e dopo la guerra*, degree dissertation, University of Turin; published by Tipografica Salesiana, Milan.

Sraffa, Piero (1922a) 'The bank crisis in Italy', *Economic Journal*, vol. 32, pp. 178–197.

Sraffa, Piero (1922b) 'L'attuale situazione delle banche italiane', *Manchester Guardian Commercial — The Reconstruction of Europe*, vol. 11, pp. 694–695.

Sraffa, Piero (1925) 'Sulle relazione fra costo e quantita prodotta', *Annali i Economica*, vol. 3. no. 1, pp. 277–328.
Sraffa, Piero (1926) 'The laws of returns under competitive conditions', *Economic Journal*, vol. 36, pp. 535–550.
Sraffa, Piero (1930) '"A criticism" and "a rejoinder"', *Economic Journal*, vol. 40, pp. 89–92 and p. 93.
Sraffa, Piero (1932) 'Dr Hayek on money and capital', *Economic Journal*, vol. 42, pp. 42–53.
Sraffa, Piero (1951) with the collaboration of Maurice Dobb, *Works and Correspondence of David Ricardo*, vol. 1, Cambridge University Press.
Sraffa, Piero (1960) *Production of Commodities by Means of Commodities: Prelude to a Critique of Economic Theory*, Cambridge University Press.
Sraffa, Piero (1961) 'Comment', in F.A. Lutz and D.C. Hague (eds) *The Theory of Capital*, Macmillan, pp. 305–306.
Sraffa, Piero (1962) '*Production of commodities: a comment*', *Economic Journal*, vol. 72, pp. 477–479.
Strachey, John (1935) *The Nature of Capitalist Crisis*, Victor Gollanz.

4

The Economics of Michal Kalecki

MALCOLM SAWYER

In some circles Michal Kalecki is regarded as among the greatest economists of the twentieth century. David Worswick, former Director of the National Institute of Economic and Social Research (London) has written 'I thought him [Kalecki] the best [economist in the world] when I knew him in the war, and I still think so' (Worswick 1977). Geoff Harcourt has described him as 'the most neglected of all great modern economists' (Harcourt 1975). Yet in many circles, particularly neoclassical ones, he is virtually unheard of or discussed. As I hope I shall make clear below, Kalecki always operated outside the neoclassical tradition, so that the ignorance of his work by mainstream economists is perhaps not surprising. I want to begin by giving a brief biography of Kalecki, which will highlight the influences on his work in the area of economics. Most of the paper will focus on some key features of his approach to economics, with some illustrations of how these features influenced his analysis.

Brief Biography

Michal Kalecki was born in 1899 into a Polish Jewish family in Lodz (Poland) then occupied by Russia. His academic training was in engineering and after an interruption for military service his formal education was brought to an end by his father's unemployment. His background in engineering gave him a good grounding in mathematics and he was self-taught in economics. As a consequence he was exposed to the neoclassical (Walrasian general equilibrium) ideas then dominant in Polish academic circles only at a relatively late stage and his early studies of economics were of the ideas of, *inter alia*, Rosa Luxemburg, Tugan-Baranovski and Marx.

Kalecki's work during the 1920s covered a range of jobs from making credit ratings of firms applying for loans to undertaking market research and economics journalism. He was also involved in political journalism and maintained a close connection with left-wing socialist movements. In the inter-war period Poland suffered from heavy unemployment and this strongly influenced Kalecki's political thinking as well as his economic analysis. In late 1929 he obtained his first quasi-academic employment at the Research Institute of Business Cycles and Prices in Warsaw. His early work at this institute covered reports on specific industries, often with a focus on those which involved monopoly or cartels (which I think influenced his general outlook on industry and his stress on the degree of monopoly in an industry). A major project with which Kalecki was involved at the Institute was the pioneering preparation of estimates of national income and its components.

Another feature of Kalecki's work at the Institute is indicated in its title: the study of business cycles. The focus on the determination of monopoly/oligopoly prices, on national income aggregates and the importance of the study of the business cycle remained throughout Kalecki's work on the macroeconomics of capitalism. His initial (and also his later) work in economics was practical in the sense that it dealt with issues of current relevance. While he dealt with those issues in a theoretical as well as an empirical way, his interest in theory was nevertheless an aid to understanding the operations of an actual economy.

In 1933 he published a paper in Polish under the title of 'Outline of a theory of the business cycle' (Kalecki 1933), later translated into English as part of *Studies in the Theory of the Business Cycle: 1933–1939* (1966; reprinted as Kalecki 1971, Chapter 1), in which he presented the basic idea of the importance of fluctuations in investment expenditure as a generator of business cycles. This and some related papers (e.g. those included in *Studies in the Theory of the Business Cycle,* reprinted as Kalecki 1971, Chapters 1 to 3) form the basis of the claim that Kalecki published some of the key ideas of Keynes before Keynes himself did so (1933 versus 1936). The key ideas which they share are the relevance of the level of aggregate demand, investment demand as the key element in aggregate demand and the idea that real wages are not determined in the labour market (see below). Although there are some similarities in their approaches, the general view which I have argued elsewhere (Sawyer 1985, Chapter 9) is that there are very substantial differences in both their framework of analysis (for example, Kalecki adopted an oligopolistic framework whereas Keynes adopted an atomistic competitive one) and in their specific analysis (for example, Kalecki assumed an endogenous money supply determined by the banking system and the demand for loans whereas in the *General Theory* (Keynes 1936), Keynes assumed as exogenous money supply whose volume was determined by the central bank).

At the time of publication of the *General Theory* (February 1936), Kalecki was travelling in Sweden on a Rockefeller Foundation fellowship. When Kalecki relised the significance of Keynes's ideas for his own research, he delayed writing a book developing his own ideas. In April 1936 he travelled to England and spent much time at the London School of Economics and at Cambridge where he made contact with Keynes, Joan Robinson and others. 'Keynes did not sympathize with Kalecki's political presuppositions and by background and temperament they could not have been further apart. I commented on this once, saying "oil and vinegar would not mix"' (Robinson 1977a).

During the war Kalecki, along with a number of other refugees from Eastern European countries (many of whom became well-known in the post-war period), was employed at the Oxford University Institute of Statistics. In this period Kalecki undertook some important independent work as well as contributing to the commentary on current economic policy published at three-weekly intervals by the Institute. The commentaries of Kalecki show a general feature of his approach to economics: the interplay between theorising and observation of reality, combined with a concern for the 'underdog' and the pursuit of social justice. Kalecki's work during this period covered writings on the prospects of the post-war economy, including the socio-political difficulties of maintaining full employment and the limits on the use of investment stimulation as a means of achieving full employment.

At the end of 1946, Kalecki was appointed, with the approval of the Polish authorities, as Deputy Director of a section of the economics department of the United Nations secretariat. His stay at the UN ended in 1954 with his resignation, which was his answer to restrictions placed on himself and others by the McCarthyism which was then sweeping the USA.

From the beginning of 1955 until his death in 1970 Kalecki's home was in Poland. The first two years of his return to Poland coincided with the growth of overt political opposition to the Polish government, the Poznan workers' uprising in June 1956 and the spread of strikes across Poland, and the spontaneous creation of workers' councils in October 1956 (the Polish October). In an environment of discontent with centralised planning and the emphasis on rapid industrialisation, Kalecki was heavily involved in the debates over the roles of decentralisation, workers' councils, the speed of industrialisation and the relative size of consumption and investment. In those debates, Kalecki took a characteristically independent line. He came into conflict with the authorities when he advocated that more attention should be paid to consumption and less to investment (thereby producing a lower rate of growth). However, he did not have great enthusiasm for decentralisation or the use of market mechanisms, a view advocated by many economists in Poland, in part as a reaction to the problems confronted by centralised planning. 'He did not ... oppose the idea of utilizing the market mechanism, but considered it a subordinate element in the running of an economy which should be planned centrally as far as the main lines of development were concerned' (Brus 1977).

In the second half of the 1950s, Kalecki was Chairman of the Commission of Perspective Planning; but his official role effectively ended in 1960. In the last decade of his life, Kalecki was heavily involved with problems of economic development and helped organise seminars at the Academy of Sciences, Warsaw University and the Central School for Planning and Statistics.

By 1968 the political climate in Poland had changed considerably for the worse from the climate of relatively free discussion in the late 1950s. Kalecki's outspokenness, disagreement with the heavy industry investment programme (and elements of anti-Semitism) brought him into disfavour. Many of his followers and colleagues were purged from office and employment (many eventually left Poland), though Kalecki's fame and age protected him from the worst of the authorities' actions against his followers.

Kalecki's career pattern was not that of a typical academic largely working in a university environment; he worked in research institutes, international organisations and planning bodies. He was often concerned with current economic problems, which he approached by seeking to combine theoretical insights with analysis based on assumptions which reflected the key elements of the problem under review.

Kalecki's Approach to Economics

Kalecki made significant contributions to the economic analysis of industrialised capitalist economies, of centrally planned economies and of developing economies. It is not possible to cover all these contributions in the space of a single chapter and I have decided to focus on his analysis of industrialised capitalist economies. In doing so, I hope to illustrate key features of Kalecki's analysis, not only for the purposes of writing intellectual history but also for their current relevance.

In one sense Kalecki adopted different analyses for each of these three types of economies. For example, he argued that unemployment in capitalist economies was generally the result of inadequate aggregate demand in the presence of plentiful capital equipment. But unemployment in developing economies was thought to arise mainly from the inadequacy of capital equipment to employ the available labour force. Centrally planned economies face problems arising from a lack of resources and productivity growth ('resource-constrained' economies), whereas developed capitalist economies were often 'demand-constrained'.

However, there is an underlying coherence. The differences of analysis arise in part from the view that different types of economies require different analyses, i.e. that there is not one general economic analysis applicable to all economies regardless of their stage of development, form of property ownership or institutional arrangements. However, there is a common element in Kalecki's analyses of different types of economy which is the interplay between economic theory and empirical observation, so that assumptions of the theory are derived from observation. Economic analysis should be set in its socio–political environment and the constraints which the latter impose on economic policy taken fully into account.

In his writings Kalecki's focus was on macroeconomics rather than microeconomics, though he did not make as sharp a division between the two as conventional economic analysis does. Even within the area of the macroeconomics of capitalist economies it is not possible to deal in depth with all aspects of Kalecki's work. I have chosen to deal with three areas which I see as providing some important insights, as relevant for current policy discussions and which constitute some of the key elements of his macroeconomics. These aspects also illustrate some general features of Kalecki's work. The areas of Kalecki's work which I will discuss are the degree of monopoly (which indicates the impact of firms' behaviour for wages and profits), the determinants of investment expenditure and the political economy of unemployment.

One common theme which appears in each of these three areas is that of economic power. In the degree of monopoly case, it is the power possessed by oligopolists in the determination of prices (relative to costs) and the consequent effects on profits and real wages. With investment, it is the power of those making investment expenditure decisions to carry through those decisions which force savings to adjust to that level of investment expenditure. In the discussion of the political economy of unemployment the emphasis is on the relative power of capitalists and workers.

Before dealing with these three general topics, it is useful to consider Kalecki's general approach to economics. His main work with which we are concerned here was in the area of economic theory. While theory obviously involves abstraction, Kalecki's theorising could be said to be rather concrete. Marx, for example, operated at different levels of abstraction and moved between different levels as appropriate to the purpose at hand. In contrast, Kalecki operated at a rather concrete level of abstraction. Kalecki was not concerned with the type of questions raised by neoclassical general equilibrium theory or by the neo-Ricardians. In those approaches abstract models are constructed within which answers are sought to questions concerning equilibrium prices, etc. and views are expressed on the source of value. Kalecki, in contrast, was concerned with the determination of actual market prices (rather than equilibrium prices such as those based on costs of production). This reflects Kalecki's concern with the behaviour of actual economies and with the analysis of major problems facing economies rather than with metaphysical questions.

Kalecki did not seek to develop an equilibrium analysis but was concerned with the movement of an economy through time (making no assumption that it was tending towards any equilibrium position). There are occasions on which Kalecki used equilibrium analysis for an individual firm or industry in the sense that firms are seen as maximising profits as far as they can (within the limitations set by rivals, demand for products and the perceptions of the firms involved). But it was individual firms rather than the whole system which were in some kind of equilibrium. While a firm could be said to be in equilibrium in the current period, the position of the firm would be changed in the next period: equilibrium is not repetitive but carries the seeds of its own destruction. For example, a firm may carry through its investment plans (and in that limited sense be in equilibrium) but make different investment plans in the next period with a different capital stock, rate of profit, etc.

In a similar vein, Kalecki saw the long-run evolution of the economy as being built up from the short-term movements of that economy. 'The long-run trend is but a slowly changing component of a chain of short-period situations' (Kalecki 1971, p. 165). In other words, the long run is not to be analysed in terms of long-run equilibrium (whether of a stationary state or in terms of balanced growth) but rather to be seen as built up from a series of short-run positions. In much of economic theory an economy is seen to move through a series of short-run (possibly equilibrium) positions en route to the long-run equilibrium position, which is unaffected by the short-run positions. In contrast, Kalecki saw the long run as having no independent existence and as being constructed from the short-run positions.

Kalecki's analysis was conducted outside the neoclassical tradition. He made virtually no use of the standard tools of neoclassical economics — the utility function, the production function, competitive markets which generally clear, and equilibrium. He had little to say about consumer behaviour (and assumed that workers spent nearly all of their income). On the production side, Kalecki usually made the working assumption that in the short run capital equipment was not easily varied and that the amount of labour and material inputs used were basically determined by the level of output. Substitution possibilities between various inputs were taken as unimportant and hence the relative prices of inputs would not influence their employment.[1] Investment (as discussed further below) in capital machinery was influenced by availability of finance, profitability and the level of demand and once again relative prices had no role to play.

Kalecki operated within the broad tradition of economic analysis which stands in opposition to neoclassical economics (which for convenience we label the classical tradition). There are a variety of approaches with the broad classical tradition. Kalecki was strongly influenced by the writings of Marx (see Sawyer 1985, Chapter 8). Many aspects of post-Keynesian economics owe much to Kalecki (and perhaps more to Kalecki than to Keynes).[2] Harcourt (1987) identifies three traditions within post-Keynesian economics, one of which is closely associated with the work of Kalecki and Joan Robinson.

In line with the classical tradition, Kalecki undertook his analysis at the level of social classes rather than the level of individuals. This leaves no role for utility analysis, which operates at the level of the individual, and it recognises that social classes have an existence over and above being a mere grouping of individuals. The classical tradition also places an emphasis on the distribution of income between social classes (in Ricardo's words, 'the principal problem of political economy'), and the role of income distribution in Kalecki's schema will be seen below. The classical tradition also stresses growth and the creation of resources rather than the allocation of resources, which has been a major concern of neoclassical economics. This is reflected below in the discussion of investment (creation of new sources). Kalecki viewed investment as important both as a component of aggregate demand and as a major force behind economic growth.

Kalecki was a political economist in the broadest sense of that term. His interest in economic analysis sprang from a desire to understand and change the world and his writings always dealt with questions of practical importance (e.g. determination of levels of unemployment and of economic growth rates). His analysis made assumptions which reflected his view of the important aspects of the question at hand. His analysis was cognisant of the socio-political constraints on economic policy. This will be illustrated below in discussion of the political economy of full employment and is very evident in his writings on developing economies (Kalecki 1976, see also Sawyer 1985, Chapter 10). In both cases there were seen to be some social classes who would lose from change (e.g. pursuit of full employment, land reform) and they would use their social and political power to try and prevent the implementation of such changes.

Kalecki's ideas form a coherent approach to macroeconomics. In outlining his approach I will start with the behaviour of firms, which make two key sets of decisions relating to price and to investment. Prices are set by firms in pursuit of profits and the extent to which firms can raise prices above costs depends on the degree of market power which they possess. The price–cost margin serves to set the real (product) wage of workers, since wage is part of costs and the relationship between wages and prices (the real product wage) is set when the price–cost margin is set. Further, at a given level of output, the price–cost margin determines the volume of profits and thereby the rate of profit of capital.

The distribution of income between wages and profits which is set by the price–cost margin is important for the level of aggregate demand. The propensity to save out of profits is much greater than that out of wages. Further, both the size of profits and the rate of profitability influence the rate of investment. Investment is a particularly important element of aggregate demand, and one liable to considerable fluctuations, which in turn generate fluctuations of economic activity, including employment.

This brief description of Kalecki's approach should highlight two aspects. The first is the key role given to aggregate demand rather than relative prices in the determination of employment and output. The second is that capitalist firms play the dominant role in making the crucial decisions on investment and price and labour plays a subsidiary role.

The Degree of Monopoly, Prices and Real Wages

The notion of the degree of monopoly is at the same time the best known aspect of Kalecki's work and the most misunderstood.[3] I would describe the idea of the degree of monopoly as follows. The degree of monopoly in an industry (or in more appealing phraseology the extent of market power or the degree of oligopoly power) depends on factors such as the degree of concentration among firms, the extent of effective collusion among them, the conditions of entry into the industry and the level of product differentiation. Each of these factors helps to secure the position of existing firms and to permit prices to be raised relative to costs. The extent of collusion and entry is not mechanically determined by the level of concentration or barriers to entry but also depends on the previous history of the industry concerned. The degree of monopoly in an industry will be reflected in the extent to which prices are above marginal costs.

Let us write this as:

$$(p - mc)/p = f(X) \tag{1}$$

where p is price, mc marginal costs and X a vector of terms reflecting market power as listed above. This equation reflects the intuitively appealing idea that the greater the market power, the larger the mark up of price over marginal costs. Formal models (e.g. Cowling 1982) have been developed which yield very similar outcomes.

There are many important aspects of this approach which I would like to highlight. First, equation (1) should indicate that Kalecki's degree of monopoly approach is a theory, in the sense that it produces potentially refutable predictions. In other words, equation (1) can be estimated provided that the elements of X can be measured and a judgement can be made as to whether the predictions of the theory do or do not hold. Indeed, some recent work has been concerned with testing the degree of monopoly approach (e.g. Reynolds 1984). Much empirical work on the relationship between industrial structure and profitability in industrial economics has involved variables similar to those mentioned by Kalecki.

The charge that Kalecki's degree of monopoly approach was a tautology rather than a theory was based on aspects of its presentation. The term 'degree of monopoly' was sometimes used so as to be coincident with the mark up of price over marginal costs, whereas the mark up should be seen as a consequence of the degree of monopoly.

Second, the degree of monopoly approach, by its title as well as its content, clearly views developed capitalist economies as essentially oligopolistic. Kalecki viewed the concept of perfect competition 'as a most unrealistic assumption' which 'when its actual status of a handy model is forgotten becomes a dangerous myth' (Kalecki 1971, p. 158). The rejection of the concept of perfect competition applies to the product market for industrial goods and services (which is our concern here), the labour market (where collective bargaining and trade unions are seen as important features) and financial markets. In each case the rejection of perfect competition and the use of an oligopolistic approach leads to a fundamental change in the analysis. For example, in the case of financial markets, instead of firms being able to borrow as much as they like at the prevailing rate of interest (one aspect of the competitive market assumption), the cost of finance depends on, *inter alia*, the firm's previous profitability record.

Kalecki's rejection of the model of perfect competition as a useful way of understanding the real world was based on both theoretical and empirical arguments. On the theoretical plane, he was strongly influenced by Sraffa's 1926 article, in which he had pointed out the incompatibility between perfect competition and decreasing unit costs (since decreasing costs would encourage the growth of monopoly), combined with the observation that firms were often operating subject to decreasing costs. On the empirical side, Kalecki's research on industries in Poland had often focused on the existence of monopoly power and cartels. Thus, as an empirical matter, monopolies and cartels were important in the industrial sector.

Kalecki drew a distinction between cost-determined prices and demand-determined prices. Cost-determined prices, which are those considered under the heading of the degree of monopoly, are those prices which change largely as a consequence of movements in costs with demand changes having little direct impact on prices. Industrial products and many services would fall into this category. The idea that price changes are largely determined by cost changes and are little affected by the level of or changes in demand follows easily from Kalecki's analysis.

Products whose prices were demand-determined are mainly raw materials and foodstuffs. The 'sector of basic raw materials [conform] in their price formation to that of perfect competition' (Kalecki 1971, p. 161) in the sense that prices change in response to demand. However, the focus of Kalecki's analysis was on the cost-determined prices which were seen as of predominant importance within developed economies. Thus, raw materials can be seen as either supplied from outside the developed economies or subject to price control.

Third — although this was not an integral part of the degree of monopoly approach — Kalecki in his presentation of that approach was one of the first to make the working assumption that firms (in the industrial sector) operated subject to approximately constant variable costs up to physical capacity. Firms then operated subject to decreasing total costs (since average fixed costs would decrease with output). Constant average variable cost implies, of course, that marginal and average variable costs are equal, an assumption which has been widely followed in industrial economics literature. The assumption of constant marginal costs reinforces the rejection of perfect competition since the level of output of a perfectly competitive firm becomes indeterminate with constant marginal costs. For convenience of exposition, I will adopt this assumption of constant average variable costs, so that (1) can be written as:

$$p = ac/(1 - f(X)) \tag{2}$$

where *ac* is average variable costs.

Fourth, the degree of monopoly approach places firms at the centre of attention in the determination of prices, rather than leaving price determination to an anonymous market or to an auctioneer. Profits are seen as arising from the exercise of market power: in the absence of some market power profits would disappear. The share of profits is therefore seen to depend upon the extent of that market power. With the substitution of *ac* for *mc* in (1) and multiplication of numerator and denominator of the lefthand side by the level of output we have:

$$(p - ac).q/p.q = f(\mathrm{X}) \tag{3}$$

and the excess of sales revenue (*p.q*) over variables costs (*ac.q*) covers fixed ('unmarked up') costs and profits. Thus we have:

$$(P + F)/S = f(X) \tag{4}$$

where *P* is total profits, *F* fixed costs and *S* sales. Thus the share of profits in sales is dependent upon the degree of monopoly and the extent of fixed costs.

At the aggregate level, the sales (gross output) of domestic firms are equal to domestic net output (value-added) plus imported inputs. For each industry the material inputs are separated into domestic and imported inputs and domestic inputs are decomposed into labour and material inputs. A simple manipulation defines the share of profits in national income as:

$$(P + F)/NO = f(X).(W + M)/(W + f(X).\mathrm{M}) \qquad (5)$$

where NO is domestic net output (W, F and P), M imported material inputs and $f(X)$ is a weighted average of industry's mark up. Thus the key determinants for the share of profits (and thereby share of wages) in national income become the degree of monopoly and the relationship between imported material inputs and domestic wages.

The fifth implication, and in respect of current macroeconomic concern perhaps the most important conclusion, relates to the determination of, and movements in, real wages. Average variable costs can be expanded as $(wL + mM)/Q$ where w is money wage, m price of inputs, L use of labour and M of material inputs. Manipulation of (2) with the substitution for average variable costs yields as the real product wage:

$$w/p = (1 - f)\ Q/L - mM/pL \qquad (6)$$

This applies at the level of industry and we assume that an analogous relationship will hold at the aggregate level. Then m becomes the price of imported materials. It could be anticipated that imported industrial goods would compete with domestically produced industrial goods. Thus the competition from foreign goods could to some extent be expected to influence the degree of monopoly. The extent is likely to depend on the relationships between 'domestic' firms and 'foreign' firms; there may, for example, be collusion between such firms or the firms may be under common ownership (i.e. be multinational enterprises).

One conclusion which can be drawn from equation (6) is that money wages may be set by collective bargaining or otherwise; but *real* wages are determined by the interplay of those money wages and the prices set by the degree of monopoly and imported material prices. This strongly suggests that firms 'have the last word' in the determination of real wages. Trade unions seeking to raise real wages would need to modify the degree of monopoly (reflected in the $f(X)$ term if they were to be successful. Rapid rises in money wages in a particular sector may have that effect since that sector would be at a price disadvantage compared with other sectors if its prices rose sufficiently to reflect the increased money wages in that sector. However, it should be recognised that little is said about the objectives of trade unions and workers in this approach. If, for example, trade unions aimed for wages to be a particular share of output which conflicted with that indicated by the degree of market power possessed by the firms, than the scene would be set for a wage–price spiral as each side tried to achieve its aims.

The movement of real wages over the course of a business cycle can also be inferred from equation (6). The movement of real wages can be seen to depend on movements in f (reflecting the degree of monopoly), Q/L (labour productivity), m/p (imported material input price to domestic prices) and M/L (ratio of materials to labour input). Thus, for example, if during a slump firms compete more intensively then f would fall and it can be seen from (1) that price–cost margins would also tend to fall and from (4) that the real wage would tend to rise. In those circumstances we would observe higher real wages and lower employment. But clearly there would be no implication that higher real wages were the *cause* of low levels of employment or that cutting wages would be a way of restoring full employment.

Within Kalecki's approach there are strong reasons for thinking that real wages would not vary greatly during the course of the trade cycle. The degree of monopoly, labour productivity and the ratio of labour to materials could all be expected to show considerable, though not complete, stability. The movement of imported material prices to domestic prices would be expected to depend upon movements in the (domestic) exchange rate and the general world material input price level. For example, a world recession would be expected to reduce world material prices (since they are seen as being demand-determined), thereby raising domestic real wages.

In Kalecki's view prices are set (given wages, etc.) to achieve firms' objectives. Thus, provided that profits are above some minimum necessary level, firms can be presumed willing to offer the employment necessary to produce the required output whatever the real wage. The main effect of a rise in real wages (relative to productivity) and a decrease in the degree of monopoly would *not* be directly on employment and output but rather operate indirectly through the effect on profits and thereby on investment, as will be discussed in the next section.

There are a number of other issues connected with the degree of monopoly which could be dealt with here. But in my view they are of less direct relevance to current macroeconomics debates than the points indicated above. However I have dealt with these other issues elsewhere (Sawyer 1985, Chapters 2 and 12).

The above analysis has important implications for macroeconomic analysis. In particular, it suggests that industrial prices are largely cost-determined and that the reduction of money and real wages will do much to reduce unemployment. These implications flow easily from the use of the idea of the 'degree of monopoly'. The difference between Kalecki's analysis and that of much mainstream macroeconomic theory arises from the use of an oligopolistic framework, in which firms have significant market power, instead of the use of a perfectly competitive approach.

Investment and Aggregate Demand

Throughout his writings on capitalist economies, Kalecki saw investment expenditure as being crucially important. The links between investment and the business cycle were the subject of his first major papers (Kalecki 1935a, 1935b) and of one of his last (Kalecki 1968); this indicates his 'continual search for new solutions in the theory of investment decisions' (Kalecki 1971, p. viii). He regarded the 'determination of investment decisions by, broadly speaking, the level and the rate of change of economic activity ... [as] the central *pièce de résistance* of economics' (Kalecki 1971, p. 165).

Kalecki's theories on investment expenditure are built on a number of key assumptions on the characteristics of investment and on objectives and constraints facing firms. Perhaps the most important one is the general view of investment expenditure as the active component of aggregate demand, with consumer expenditure seen as the passive component. Investment expenditure is seen not as *determined* by current income but rather as *determining* the level of income, whereas consumer expenditure is largely constrained by the level of consumers' income. Investment expenditure and savings are (in a simple closed private economy) equal *ex post*; but Kalecki saw investment expenditure as causing (forcing) savings. Firms make investment plans for some future time period, which are largely carried out and to which savings have to adjust in order that the national income accounts identities can hold. But the manner in which savings and investment are brought into equality is through the level of economic activity changing. So far so Keynesian; but we now turn to Kalecki's specific contributions.

We begin with the apparently unimportant point that a distinction is drawn between decisions and the implementation of investment expenditure. This allows Kalecki to model current economic variables as influencing the investment decisions which in turn lead at some future date to actual investment expenditure. Since investment decisions are planned to be implemented in the future, with allowance made for delays in obtaining finance, in the construction of capital equipment, etc., those decisions can be viewed as by and large carried out, though with some significant time lag.

The finance for investment for a firm comes from a combination of internal funds and external borrowing. Firms have a preference for internal funds, which arises in part from the view that internal funds are less costly in a variety of ways than external funds. The use of external funds involves the various transactions costs of raising the loan or making new share issues. The volume of internal funds available to a firm will be largely determined by the volume of profits, so that current profits (or perhaps more accurately cash flow) are an important determinant of investment.

The use of external funds by a firm is eventually limited by the increasing costs of such funds as the amount of external funds required by a firm increases. Kalecki introduced 'the principle of increasing risk' (Kalecki 1937). In effect, the argument is that the greater the volume of borrowing which a firm wishes to undertake (relative to its profits and assets), the greater the risk that it will be unable to repay the interest charges and the capital sum itself. Financial institutions take this increasing risk into account and charge higher rates of interest for larger volumes of borrowing.

The volume of borrowing by a firm is therefore likely to be strongly influenced by its profits. The constraints imposed by the availability of finance on the expansion of a firm were seen by Kalecki as particularly important. 'The size of a firm thus appears to be circumscribed by the amount of its entrepreneurial capital both through its influence on the capacity to borrow capital and through its effect on the degree of risk' (Kalecki 1971, p. 106). The limitations on the size of the firm may be short-term limits on the rate of expansion, since as time passes profits accrue which may enable the firm to expand further by the use of internal finance and external finance secured on the basis of its profits.

For firms collectively investment expenditures are constrained by the available finance, which in turn is constrained by the available pool of savings and the willingness of banks to create 'new' money. Investment decisions are strongly influenced by the savings available now, though those decisions will lead to levels of future investment expenditure and thereby to future savings levels. When a particular volume of investment expenditure has taken place it will generate (in a closed private economy) the corresponding amount of savings. But those savings are available only after investment has taken place and are not available to finance that investment. The finance for that investment has to come from previous savings and the creation of credit by banks. In Kalecki's analysis it was assumed that banks could, and generally would, create loans and thereby add to the stock of money. His assumptions on this were often tucked away as footnotes and he did not place any great stress on them. Nor did he analyse what happened to the money after it was created. The firm taking out the loan (and hence initially holding the increase of the money stock) would spend the money on its investment and the money would pass to others. In some cases it could be expected that the money would be passed on again but in other cases used to repay outstanding loans thereby reducing the money supply (cf Kaldor 1982, Asimakopulos 1983).

Kalecki clearly saw that it was a condition for expansion of aggregate demand that loans were granted to finance that increase in demand. Investment expenditure above the prevailing level of savings could occur only if banks were willing to finance the increased investment expenditure. He generally assumed as a first approximation that loans to finance investment would be granted by the banks so that the investment could proceed. The extent of those loans would be limited by the desire of firms to borrow to finance investment rather than by the desire of banks to extend loans. Kalecki recognised that there could be times when banks would respond to increased demand for loans by raising the rate of interest on loans, thereby choking off the demand and so the planned increase in investment expenditure. But he did not analyse the situations in which banks would extend further loans and those in which they would raise interest rates on loans.

It is notable that Kalecki always saw money as being predominantly created by the banking system in response to the demand for loans. In recent jargon, he saw the money stock as endogenously determined (by the interaction between firms and banks) and money as being largely 'inside money'.

Investment expenditure is seen as conditional on the availability of finance, which in turn is set by the existing level of savings and the willingness or otherwise of banks to lend. But we now need to turn to the influences directly at work on investment expenditures. One rather general way of looking at Kalecki's approach is to ask why a firm would wish to increase its capital stock, i.e. to make a positive net investment.

First, in each time period, finance becomes available as profits are made and savings undertaken. Thus some potential investment delayed in the past because of a lack of finance can now proceed as finance becomes available. Second, the incentive for a firm to own and operate capital equipment can be expected to depend on the prospective rate of profit on that capital equipment relative to the rate of interest at which the firm can borrow. A change in the relationship between the average rate of profit and the average rate of interest on borrowing would generate a change in the desired stock of capital equipment owned by firms and thus generate investment. But Kalecki saw the level of long-term interest rates (which are significant for investment decisions) as rather stable. He therefore saw changes in the rate of profit as generating investment. The rate of profit would change either because profits changed or because the capital stock changed. The latter would automatically change when non-zero net investment occurred. The former would arise from, *inter alia*, fluctuations in the level of output (and thereby profits) and in the degree of monopoly (influencing the profits-to-sales ratio).

Investment expenditure at some time in the near future is seen as related to the current level of savings (which, in a simple economy, would equal current investment expenditure), the rate of change of profits and the change in the capital stock.

Net investment would come to an end when firms had the capital equipment they required. Kalecki argued that a positive rate of technical progress would be necessary to prevent the economy reaching a stationary state (zero growth) and that the faster the underlying rate of technical progress the higher the level of investment expenditure (relative to GDP). This could easily lead on to the view that there could be long-term fluctuations in investment which arose from fluctuations in the underlying rate of technical progress. Thus there could be periods of time when a major breakthrough (e.g. steam propulsion) generated a high level of investment, whereas in other periods research and development would be unrewarding and investment low. Since investment is the key active component of aggregate demand, this would lead to recession.

In effect, for a fully employed economy, there has to be the right balance between the degree of monopoly and the level of investment. The degree of monopoly serves to determine (given foreign prices and fixed costs) the share of profits in net output. At the full employment level of output a particular level of savings would be generated, depending upon the division of income as between wages and profits, which in turn would depend on the degree of monopoly and the propensity to save out of the two types of income. For full employment to be secured the level of investment would have to equal the level of savings.

There is one crucial difference between Kalecki's approach to investment and that of Keynes and of neoclassical economists. Keynes's approach to investment started from the notion that a firm would wish to adjust its capital stock until there was an equality between the 'marginal efficiency of capital', with a fixed rate of interest so far as the firm itself was concerned. This rate of interest would differ between firms, depending on their risk rating. The demand for capital equipment by a firm is then derived as a (negative) function of the rate of interest (and also the state of expectations, which are important to Keynes's work but which are not central to our argument here; so following Keynesian economics we place emphasis on the rate of interest rather than the state of expectations). The aggregate investment schedule is then derived by the summation of individual firms' investment schedules.

In his review of the *General Theory* Kalecki made two particular criticisms of Keynes's approach. First, he argued that Keynes's approach related to the demand for a stock of capital equipment and said nothing about the speed with which the firm would adjust its actual capital stock to the desired level. In other words it said little about the *rate* of investment. In the work of Kalecki there is a constraint on the rate of investment which arises from the financial side, as indicated above.

Second, the marginal efficiency of capital (or more generally, the forces influencing a firm's investment decisions) depends on the general level of investment. If firms collectively plan to invest more in a future period than they are currently doing, then in that future period demand, and hence profits, will be higher as a result of that higher investment. The marginal efficiency of capital will then have risen and firms will again plan to increase investment. Keynes and the neoclassical economists omit this cumulative aspect of investment.

The approach Kalecki adopted was to seek to model aggregate investment directly by building in constraints which applied at the aggregate level rather than by modelling individual firms' investment decisions and then aggregating them. The particular constraint which is built in relates to the availability of finance.

We can summarise the points in Kalecki's approach to investment which are of wider significance than the modelling of investment decisions. These include:

(i) the macro-aggregate approach;
(ii) the financial constraints on individual firms and firms collectively;
(iii) the active and fluctuating nature of investment;
(iv) (though perhaps not particularly important here) the oligopolistic nature of firms.

The Political Economy of Full Employment

In the last few years of the war Kalecki contributed extensively to discussions on the prospects for the post-war economy and for avoiding the recurrence of mass unemployment. In one sense he was rather pessimistic about the prospects for full employment. He foresaw considerable difficulties arising from international trade problems, in particular from imbalances between countries and the difficulties in removing balance-of-payments deficits without resort to deflation. He was among those who saw a substantial gap between full employment income and consumer expenditure which would have to be filled by investment and government expenditure if full employment was to be achieved.

There was only one sense in which Kalecki could be said to have been optimistic about the post-war prospects. He argued (Kalecki 1944b) that 'government expenditure on public investment and subsidies to mass consumption ... is *always* capable of securing full employment' (italics added). Governments now had full employment within their grasp. However, there might be difficulties arising from international trade (e.g. balance-of-payments constraints) which could prevent the achievement of full employment. But apart from international trade (the problems of which he regarded as 'perhaps the greatest *practical* difficulty in the achievement of full employment' (Kalecki 1944b)) Kalecki pointed to two constraints on the continual achievement of full employment.

The first constraint arose from limits on the manipulation of aggregate demand. Apart from foreign trade, we can talk in terms of three components of aggregate demand — consumer expenditure, investment expenditure and government expenditure. Consumer expenditure could be raised through a change in the distribution of income towards wage earners and the poor. But this was a course of action generally favoured by Kalecki as much for its social benefits as its economic ones. Kalecki saw virtually all wages as being spent, so that it would be difficult to raise the propensity to consume out of wages but perhaps possible to distribute more income in the direction of wages. But here, as with a number of redistributive policies, while they could be viewed as beneficial from an economic or social welfare perspective, there would nevertheless be strong political constraints on governments undertaking them.

Investment expenditure could be encouraged by government subsidy, lower interest rates, etc., but after a while would run into a number of difficulties. There is a level of net investment which would increase the stock of capital equipment at the same rate as output, thereby maintaining the existing capital–output ratio. An attempt to promote a higher rate of investment would lead to a mixture of excess capacity and capital deepening, i.e. a rising capital–output ratio. Unless the share of profits in output rose in sympathy, the effective rising capital–output ratio would imply a falling rate of profit. Then, in order to maintain investment levels, more subsidies would be needed to offset the declining rate of profit, which would tend to dampen down investment. This argument can be qualified in a number of ways: e.g. the rate of growth of output could rise with more investment and there is a floor to the rising capital–output ratio. But the point here is that Kalecki was sceptical about the efficacy of raising investment expenditure to ensure full employment. He also thought that it was rather wasteful in that:

> [t]he proper role of private investment is to provide tools for the production of consumption goods and not to provide enough work to employ all available labour ... Both public and private investment should be carried out only to the extent to which they are considered useful. If the effective demand thus generated fails to provide full employment, the gap should be filled by increasing consumption and not by piling up unwanted public or private equipment [Kalecki 1944b].

The limits on the net effect of government expenditure arise simply from the constraints of a rising national debt to income ratio and the consequent rising interest charges. It can also be noted here that Kalecki was critical of the 1944 White Paper on full employment for not grasping the nettle that full employment might well require a permanent budget deficit. He argued, *inter alia*, that the White Paper took the view that over a complete trade cycle the government budget should balance even if it did not balance in each year. He thought that there was a strong possibility of prolonged deficient demand in the post-war period so that a long-term government budget deficit would be required if full employment was to be secured. But that long-term budget deficit would involve the difficulty indicated above: rising national debt and interest charges relative to GDP. Kalecki proposed an annual capital tax (essentially a broadly based wealth tax) which would be charged to finance the rising interest charges in a way which in Kalecki's view would not be deflationary.[4]

However, while Kalecki thought that the use of appropriate demand management policies could remove unemployment, in an often quoted article published in 1943 (revised version appears as Kalecki 1971, Chapter 12) he argued that 'the assumption that a Government will maintain full employment in a capitalist economy if it knows how to do it is fallacious'. Kalecki started from the view that capitalist economies would not generally generate full employment — in part because of the cyclical nature of such economies, which meant that for considerable parts of the trade cycle the economy must operate at less than full employment and capacity. The maintenance of full employment in capitalist economies would, in Kalecki's view, require substantial government intervention. A prolonged period of full employment (which would be unprecedented) underpinned by government intervention would generate significant social and political changes. A resistance to the maintenance of full employment would arise from dislike by some groups of those social and political changes and from dislike of government intervention in general. Thus the second constraint on the achievement of full employment was existing social and political institutions.

The dislike of government intervention in general was seen as arising from two considerations. First, the extension of government activity could be seen as foreshadowing the replacement of capitalism by state activity and socialism. Second, under *laissez-faire* capitalism the level of employment rests on the level of investment, which in turn depends on profitability and the 'state of confidence'. The use of government expenditure to underpin full employment reduces the role of investment and, more particularly, the roles of 'the state of confidence' and profitability. 'The social function of the doctrine of "sound finance" is to make the level of employment dependent on the "state of confidence"' (Kalecki 1971, p. 139).

Kalecki suggested that the maintenance of adequate aggregate demand could require the 'subsidising of consumption' (in effect, social security provision to increase the income of lower income groups) and involve the redistribution of income from rich to poor. It would also loosen the links between work and pay (for the working classes). There is 'a "moral" principle of the highest importance ... at stake. The fundamentals of capitalist ethics require that "you shall earn your bread in sweat" — unless you happen to have private means' (Kalecki 1971, p. 140).

The experience of the long boom in post-war capitalist economies appeared in many ways to contradict Kalecki's prognosis. The expected post-war slump after reconstruction did not occur on the scale anticipated. Some countries in the post-war period (e.g. USA and UK) soon reached and were able to maintain historically low levels of unemployment, although others (notably West Germany) took several years before achieving low levels of unemployment. The 1960s saw the closest approximation so far to full employment across developed capitalist economies. 'If anything, the Europe of the 1960s may well have been an area which, probably for the first time in recorded human history, could boast of a situation of virtual full employment' (Boltho 1982, p. 15). However, the experience of the last 15 years has shown a revival of interest in this aspect of Kalecki's work, perhaps simply because his prognosis bears a closer resemblance to post- than pre-1970 experience.

The following, written by Kalecki in 1943, could well be a description of the UK situation over the past fifteen years. The maintenance of full employment

> would cause social and political changes which would give a new impetus to the opposition of business leaders. Indeed, under a regime of permanent full employment, 'the sack' would cease to play its role as a disciplinary measure. The social position of the boss would be undermined and the self assurance and class consciousness of the working class would grow. Strikes for wage increases and improvements in conditions of work would create political tension... But 'discipline in the factories' and 'political stability' are more appreciated by the business leaders than profits. Their class instinct tells them that lasting full employment is unsound from their point of view and that unemployment is an integral part of the capitalist system [1971, pp. 140–141].[5]

There are some interesting questions to be asked about why Kalecki's prognosis does not match up with the experience of the 'long boom' but does with the post-1973 experience. A lengthy discussion would take up too much space. But I would point to the following. First, investment expenditure was much more buoyant than Kalecki foresaw. Joan Robinson, in an otherwise favourable review of Kalecki's contribution to the Oxford University Institute of Statistics (Kalecki 1944b) in the *Economic Journal* 1945, argued that Kalecki had dwelt on the lack of investment demand and overlooked the possibility of too much investment. Whereas he thought that the investment required for full employment would be greater than that required for growth considerations, for much of the post-war period the reverse was perhaps true. The benefits of favourable expectations, reinforcing the effects of initial high growth rates and the importing (as far as most economies were concerned) of American technology were high on the list of factors stimulating investment.

Second, the experience of real wages rising faster than ever before and improving social conditions (the rapid extension of the welfare state) were sufficient to ensure a quiescent workforce. It must also be remembered that while the UK achieved full employment quickly, in a number of European countries full employment did not arrive until the early 1960s.

Third, the experience of the inter-war period, with high levels of unemployment and the smashing of trade unions in many countries, had a strong influence on the aspirations and behaviour of workers. It was only in the late 1960s that the majority of the workforce had entered the labour market since the end of the war. As the effects of the inter-war period wore off so the effects predicted by Kalecki became more evident.

This discussion can hope to provide only a brief introduction to Kalecki's discussions on the political economy of unemployment and full employment. In my view, the important elements in his approach are:

(i) the general presumption that unemployment and under-utilisation of capacity is the norm in developed *laissez-faire* capitalist economies;
(ii) the maintenance of full employment is technically possible following the discoveries on the importance of the level of aggregate demand but would generally require substantial government intervention in the workings of the economy;
(iii) but intervention by government and the experience of prolonged full employment would generate social and political pressures undermining full employment.

In sum, we can say that Kalecki saw full employment as altering the balance of economic power as between capital and labour:

> [F]ull employment capitalism will have, of course, to develop new social and political institutions which will reflect the increased power of the working class. If capitalism can adjust itself to full employment a fundamental reform will have been incorporated in it. If not, it will show itself an outmoded system which must be scrapped [Kalecki 1943].

Concluding Remarks

The work of Kalecki (and most other economists) can be seen as combining a general mode of analysis with a number of specific assumptions which are intended to reflect the key features of the economy under examination. I have sought to select aspects of Kalecki's work which would bring out both the nature of the general mode of analysis which he applied and some of the specific assumptions which he made.

Kalecki's specific analysis reflected the views on the nature of capitalist economies. But he was clear that there were important differences between economies. He sought to 'develop the idea that the institutional framework of a social system is a basic element of its economic dynamics and thus of the theory of growth relevant to that system' (Kalecki 1970) and, in particular, that there were substantial differences in the theories of growth applicable to *laissez-faire* capitalist economies, centrally planned economies and to 'mixed' economies. In a similar vein, Kalecki indicated that '[t]he economic development affects profoundly the state of natural resources ... the productive relations and the superstructure [social phenomena such as government, culture, science and technology]' (Kalecki 1965).

It would follow from these ideas that there is a need to consider how the specific assumptions of Kalecki's analysis should be changed to reflect the conditions of the 1980s rather than those of the 1930s. There have been changes in the balance of power between labour and capital, perhaps as foreseen by Kalecki, as a result of a long period of full employment. Concentration of firms has generally continued to increase but the growth of international trade may have had some modifying effects on the degree of monopoly. The extent of formal cartelisation is much lower than in the 1930s, although it is a moot point whether competition has changed its form and in some sense increased. The growth of workers' savings (largely in the form of compulsory contributions to pension funds) would change some of the specifics of Kalecki's analysis (as the simplifying assumption of no net savings by workers was often made).

But the most outstanding difference in the area of macroeconomics since the original writings of Kalecki and Keynes is the internationalisation of economic activity. This has taken the form of the rise of multinational enterprises, the growth of international trade in finished manufactured products and dramatic changes in foreign exchange markets (move to quasi-floating exchange rates and increased financial flows across exchanges).

There have been many significant developments in developed capitalist economies since Kalecki's main work was undertaken. Many of those developments (for example, growth of multinationals, developments of the financial system) have made Kalecki's approach more rather than less relevant. Perhaps more importantly, his style of analysis, with its emphasis on dealing with important problems, the use of realistic assumptions and the abandonment of equilibrium analysis, will continue to attract attention.

Notes

1. In his analysis of growth in a socialist economy (1972), Kalecki did make use of a function rather like a production function. This could be seen as being rather like a set of blueprints from which planners and others could make a choice.
2. I have argued elsewhere that the post-Keynesian tradition owes more to Kalecki than to Keynes (see Sawyer 1982).
3. For an extensive discussion of Kalecki's macroeconomics and the degree of monopoly in particular see Kriesler (1987).
4. The annual capital levy would be charged on all net assets (with provision to avoid double taxation) to finance the (cumulative) interest charges on the national debt in excess of the growth of national income. Kalecki argued that such a levy would not affect capitalists' consumer demand since it represented a redistribution of income from all asset holders to the holders of the national debt. Further, the levy would not affect the relative attractiveness of different assets (since all would be taxed) and hence would not adversely affect investment in capital equipment. The effective rate of return on all assets would be lowered by the capital levy. This could then lower the rate of savings. But since the economy was running a government deficit because of an excess of private savings over investment this would not be a disadvantage.
5. The following quote from the same era makes a similar point:

> The change in the workers' bargaining position which should follow from the abolition of unemployment would show itself in another and more subtle way. Unemployment in a private enterprise economy has not only the function of preserving discipline in industry, but also indirectly the function of preserving the value of money. If free wage bargaining as we have known it

hitherto, is continued in conditions of full employment, there would be a constant upward pressure upon money wage-rates. This phenomenon also exists at the present time, and is kept within bounds by the appeal of patriotism. In peace-time the vicious spiral of wages and prices might become chronic.

Taken from an article (unsigned but generally attributed to Joan Robinson) entitled 'Planning full employment—alternative solutions of a Dilemma', *The Times* 23 January 1943 as quoted in Kaldor (1983).

References

Asimakopulos, A. (1983) 'Kalecki and Keynes on finance, investment and saving', *Cambridge Journal of Economics*, vol. 7, no. 3.

Boltho, A. (1982) 'Growth' in A. Boltho (ed.), *The European Economy: Growth and Crisis*, Oxford University Press.

Brus, W. (1977) 'Kalecki's economics of socialism', *Oxford Bulletin of Economics and Statistics*, vol. 39, no. 1.

Cowling, K. (1982) *Monopoly Capitalism*, Macmillan.

Harcourt, G. C. (1975) 'Capital theory: much ado about something', *Thames Papers in Political Economy*, Autumn 1975.

Harcourt, G. C. (1987) 'Post Keynesian economics', in J. Eatwell *et al.* (eds), *The New Palgrave: A Dictionary of Economics*, Macmillan.

Kaldor, N. (1982) *The Scourge of Monetarism*, Oxford University Press.

Kaldor, N. (1983) 'Keynesian economics after fifty years', in D. Worswick and J. Trevithick (eds), *Keynes and the Modern World*, Cambridge University Press.

Kalecki, M. (1933) *Proba teorii koniunktury*, Warsaw Institute of Research on Business Cycles and Prices (translated as Kalecki (1966) Chapter 1 and reprinted as Kalecki (1971) Chapter 1.

Kalecki, M. (1935a) 'Essai d'une theorie du mouvement cyclique des affaires', *Revue d'Economie Politique*, vol. 2.

Kalecki, M. (1935b) 'A macrodynamic theory of business cycles', *Econometrica*, vol.3, no. 3.

Kalecki, M. (1937) 'Principle of increasing risk', *Economica*, vol. 4, no.4.

Kalecki, M. (1939) *Essays in the Theory of Economic Fluctuations*, Allen and Unwin.

Kalecki, M. (1943) 'Political aspects of full employment', *Political Quarterly*, vol. 14, no. 4.

Kalecki, M. (1944a) 'Professor Pigou on "The classical stationary state": a comment', *Economic Journal*, vol. 54, no. 1.

Kalecki, M. (1944b) 'Three ways to full employment', in Oxford University Institute of Statistics (1944) *The Economics of Full Employment*, Blackwell.

Kalecki, M. (1965) 'Econometric model and historical materialism', in *On Political Economy and Econometrics: Essays in Honour of Oskar Lange,* PWN, Polish Scientific Publishers.

Kalecki, M. (1966) *Studies in the Theory of the Business Cycle: 1933–39* (translated from Polish by Ada Kalecki), Blackwell.

Kalecki, M. (1968) 'Trend and the business cycle', *Economic Journal*, vol. 78, no. 2.

Kalecki, M. (1970) 'Theories of growth in different social systems', *Scientia*, nos 5–6.

Kalecki, M. (1971) *Selected Essays on the Dynamics of the Capitalist Economy*, Cambridge University Press.

Kalecki, M. (1972) *Selected Essays on the Economic Growth of the Socialist and the Mixed Economy*, Cambridge University Press.

Kalecki, M. (1976) *Essays on Developing Economies*, Harvester.

Keynes, J.M. (1936) *The General Theory of Employment, Interest and Money*, Macmillan.

Kriesler, P. (1987) *Kalecki's Microanalysis*, Cambridge University Press.

Oxford University Institute of Statistics (1945) *The Economics of Full Employment*, Blackwell.

Reynolds, P. (1984) 'An empirical analysis of the degree of monopoly theory of distribution', *Bulletin of Economic Research*, vol. 36, no. 1.

Robinson, J. (1945) 'Review of Oxford University Institute of Statistics (1945)', *Economic Journal*, vol. 55, no. 1.

Robinson, J. (1977a) 'Michal Kalecki on the economics of capitalism', *Oxford Bulletin of Economics and Statistics*, vol. 39, no. 1.

Robinson, J. (1977b) 'What are the questions?', *Journal of Economic Literature*, vol. 15, no. 4.

Sawyer, M. (1982) 'Towards a Post-Kaleckian macroeconomics', *Thames Papers in Political Economy*, Autumn 1982 (reprinted in P. Arestis and T. Skouras (eds), *Post-Keynesian Economic Theory: A Challenge to Neo-Classical Economics*, Wheatsheaf).

Sawyer, M. (1985) *The Economics of Michal Kalecki*, Macmillan.

Sraffa, P. (1926) 'The laws of return under competitive conditions', *Economic Journal*, vol. 36, no. 4.

Sraffa, P. (1960) *Production of Commodities by Means of Commodities*, Cambridge University Press.

Targetti, F. and Kinda-Hass, B. (1982) 'Kalecki's review of Keynes' *General Theory*', *Australian Economic Papers*, vol. 21, no. 4.

Worswick, G.D.N. (1977) 'Kalecki at Oxford, 1940–44', *Oxford Bulletin of Economics and Statistics*, vol. 39, no. 1.

5

From Stagnation in the 1930s to Slow Growth in the 1970s

JOSEF STEINDL

Personal Reminiscences

I should have preferred to become a biologist but that would have taken too long. So I went to business school (today called the Economic University) in Vienna. I was interested in the economics taught by Strigl, a pupil of Böhm-Bawerk, who showed me how the discussion of economic policies depended on an understanding of how the economy worked. He was a liberal and I accepted his views, preferring them to the anti-rationalist, romantic-nationalist trends which were then prominent in the university. I hated them and I hated the various Fascist movements of the time, mainly for their militarism. I felt no particular social engagement; my upbringing had been apolitical and I had no links to left-wing movements. But I could not fail to be impressed by the surrounding unemployment and misery, the more so since it affected my own position. Unemployment has remained a very important concern of mine. I soon became disaffected with the Austrian school and came under the influence of Keynes. After the German occupation I lost my job because of my hostility to the regime and I had no opportunity of pursuing a career as an economist. By great luck and with the help of the *emigré* economists (Mises, Hayek, Haberler) I obtained a stipend as a research lecturer at Balliol College. I then came to the Oxford Institute of Statistics where I was with Kalecki, whose teaching has influenced me ever since. As an economist I am the product of England and Kalecki.

These were also the years of a strong socialist conviction which in subsequent times has been sorely tried. I have hardly been influenced at all by Marx as far as pure economics, i.e. the labour value theory and all that goes with it, are concerned. I have always preferred to think of profits as the consequence of the lack of free entry which is ubiquitous and essential in capitalism in so far as you need wealth in order to set up in business, and there is a hierarchy of wealth which reserves the opportunities of exploiting the advantages of large-scale operation for those with large wealth, which is scarce. Thus profit is a differential rent, like Ricardo's positional rent. I think this is rather easier to understand than tortuous arguments about increase in working time and intensity; moreover it meets the traditional economist on his own ground.

These ideas are connected with my interest in the theory of the firm and with the role of oligopoly and concentration. I was once told that I have been referred to in Russian literature as a 'petty bourgeois economist'. Perhaps that description is not so wrong, and it is getting less wrong as time goes by. I remember that Kalecki once got furious with me because in a paper on profits I said that the small entrepreneur, being at the margin, earned no profits. He insisted on my taking this out of the paper because he did not want to exonerate any capitalists at all. It is, however, remarkable that Kalecki, although quite uncompromising in his socialist convictions, never thought on the lines of a *Katastrophenpolitik*: i.e. he never had the slightest hesitation in supporting a reformist policy of improving conditions here and now by full employment, as long as the reform improved and strengthened the position of the workers, which he was convinced was the case with full employment.

Marx's historical perspective, in contrast to his pure economics, was and is very important to me. Marx's aim was essentially to provide a rational explanation of history — history as an endogenous process in which powerful forces act on one another, some working for stability, some for change, in contrast to a view which — in its extreme form — regarded it as the work of the gods or of abstract ideas — the prototype of an 'exogenous' explanation. In this sense the starting point of my *Maturity* book was definitely Marxist: I looked for an explanation of the world depression of the 1930s with the help of whatever tools economic theory could offer (and to some extent I had to make them for myself). Mainstream economists did not find the depression easy to explain and after the war tried to forget it as quickly as possible, seeing it as a mere aberration of history. For the Marxist it was definitely more: a symptom of the basic difficulties of the system, a harbinger of its decay. But what exactly was the trouble which caused the machinery to slow down to a virtual standstill? For Kalecki, as well as for other non-doctrinaire Marxists, it was not possible, for logical and empirical reasons, to accept the Marxian explanation of the declining rate of profit. Nor could he believe Rosa Luxemburg's version of underconsumption in which the growth potential of technical change in capitalism was underrated. It remained, then, a puzzle as to why exactly the capitalist 'machine' had ceased to function and where the trouble lay. Kalecki, before he left Oxford, suggested that I should work on this. I pursued two parallel lines of approach to the problem, one centred round the problem of overcapacity, the other round finance and debt. The first theme gained more weight as the study proceeded. I asked myself what consequences for the functioning of the system would have followed from the spread of 'monopoly' elements, more precisely, of oligopoly: that is, a market structure in which a few large concerns dominate the industry and control the price, in practice often through price leadership. Once this market form comes to prevail in industry there are good grounds for speaking of a transformation of competitive capitalism, as the classics and Marx knew it, to something new: monopoly capitalism. Two eminent Marxists, Rosa Luxemburg and Rudolf Hilferding, had, each in their own way, drawn attention to this metamorphosis of capitalism which affected international relations and the political climate inside the national states.

The spread of oligopoly would do two things: (a) it would increase profit margins (at a normal level of capacity utilisation) in the oligopolistic sector of the economy, and (b) it would make the margins less flexible than before, because a few large concerns would not compete as readily as a greater number of moderately sized producers; the large concerns would be less inclined to engage in a policy of cut-throat competition which would lead to an elimination of overcapacity.

I have laid great stress on two links: the link between the rise in profit margins and/or their inflexibility and the emergence or persistence of overcapacity; and the link between overcapacity and the weakening of the incentive to invest. In a competitive economy overcapacity and excessive profit margins would be eliminated by competition, whereas in monopoly capitalism this mechanism would be impaired and accumulation and growth would therefore be weakened. In connection with these changes the capitalist system was seen as exhausting its growth potentialities gradually and in this sense becoming 'mature', as Alvin Hansen put it (1938).

I shall touch on the financial aspects only briefly. The development of the capital market (stocks and bonds) added a tremendous stimulus to growth in the ascending phase of capitalist development; but once these financial structures were established the other side of the coin became visible. A large amount of saving had been transferred from business to persons outside enterprises ('household saving'), where they did not directly contribute to stimulating investment. These savings had to be borrowed and they tended to act depressively as they grew larger. The capital market itself, instead of acting as the servant to industry, developed a life and power of its own: finance was used as an instrument of concentration, to achieve market power. This reinforced the tendencies of degeneration of the productive functions of capitalism.

My attempts to come to grips with the problem of the 'crisis of capitalism' took several years and afterwards publication was again delayed by years; when the book finally came out everybody had managed to forget all about the depression. Apart from Paul Sweezy, whose thoughts had also been directed towards the problems of monopoly and underconsumption, nobody took any notice of the book when it was published.

Stagnation Then and Now

Morishima, in a recent work (1984), has stressed that economic theory cannot be the same for every country, nor for different periods in one and the same country. This applies also to stagnation theory. My stagnation theory was to explain the secular decline of growth from the nineteenth century to the depression of the 1930s in the USA. I chose this country because it seemed to me an easier subject for study than European countries; it was more of a closed and private economy and less complicated by a feudal past and imperialism. I was, however inspired by a belief that behind the differences of individual countries a common pattern of development of accumulation in capitalism existed and that a study of a comparatively simple case might reveal something of it.

Economists in general were not much interested in my ideas because at the time of their publication the rate of accumulation and of employment was high. It was only later that interest began to increase in some circles; after 1975 I was sometimes commended for having shown foresight. This made me smile because on the one hand I did not think that the experience of post-war prosperity had necessarily disproved my ideas; on the other hand I did not think that these ideas were directly applicable to the new problems of the 1970s. Instead new explanations were required in the new situation, part of which was the change in economic policy of the early 1970s — I called it 'stagnation policy'.

I shall deal with three problems in my paper:

1. The old problem of the maturing of the American economy from the nineteenth century to the Great Depression.
2. The explanation of the exceptionally high accumulation and employment of the prosperous post-war decades and how they can be reconciled with maturity of the American economy.
3. The reasons why this prosperity period came to an end and gave way to slower growth, great unemployment and a host of subsidiary problems, such as indebtedness.

Maturity

With regard to the first of these problems I want to deal with two questions which arose from my treatment of the accumulation process in USA.

I took the view that the Great Depression of 1929-39 did not come as suddenly, from a historical perspective, as it seemed at the time: a decline in the rate of accumulation — the rate of growth of capital — had in fact begun long before. From what data we have (they are still the Kuznets data (Kuznets 1961) and they have not radically changed since), it appears that accumulation reached a high in the

1880s and declined afterwards. A decline is also apparent in the growth rate of GNP.

A first reaction to this observation might well be that the decline should not occasion any great surprise or constitute a problem, since the growth rate of the population and of the labour force had also declined. It should be regarded as only natural that the national product and the capital stock would move roughly parallel to the labour force. Before we settle, however, on this supply-determined explanation, we should consider that the accumulation process consisted largely of an enormous shift of labour from agriculture to industry and from rural to urban settlements. In fact, the growth rate of the non-agricultural labour force might be used as a primitive measure of accumulation for the early periods.

If we want to stay with a supply-determined explanation we should have to argue in the following way. The pressure of labour coming from agriculture kept wages low, which made the building up of industry and of towns possible. To the extent to which wages subsequently rose this process was later slowed down and the growth rate declined. But the fact is that real wages were high in the USA from the beginning and there was hardly any pressure from agriculture. It accords far better with what we know of the facts to say that the industrial entrepreneur had to exert a pull on the labour force by paying higher wages (which, according to E. Rothbarth (1946), also explains the comparatively great efforts of the American industrialists to introduce labour-saving innovations). This pull also affected the rate of immigration, which should not be taken as an exogenous datum but was strongly influenced by the chances of employment.

Since American development did not rely on exports but very largely depended on the internal market, the positive effects of high wages on internal demand must have outweighed the negative effects on exports. (In this respect the situation was different from that of the newly industrialising countries of more recent times.) Thus it appears plausible that the shift from agriculture was dominated by demand and that the growth of the non-agricultural labour force was the effect and not the cause of accumulation. In the same way it is highly plausible to argue that the later declining growth rate of the non-agricultural labour force was the effect of a weakening of accumulation and not its cause. The industrial labour force might well have increased more by pulling more labour out of agriculture or drawing more on foreign labour supply. The labour force was not the barrier to accumulation.

The other question I want to deal with is the role of technology. Was not, quite simply, the gradual exhaustion of the railway boom the reason for the decline of accumulation in the 1890s? The role of the railways in accumulation was no doubt considerable. I cannot, of course, uphold the view expressed in my book, that technical progress does not affect the volume of investment. I recanted long ago and maintain now, with Kalecki, that technical progress is indeed a stimulant to investment. It would be equally wrong, however, to explain accumulation entirely by the purely exogenous determinant of the rate at which new knowhow becomes available. The economic climate created by the expansion of the recent past is of decisive importance for the transformation of knowhow into innovation.

The technological explanation is speciously simple and plausible. There had to be saturation in the case of railways just as there had to be saturation with motor cars more recently, because the high expansion rates of the build-up period cannot be continued indefinitely. But the question is why other innovations have not appeared on the scene to take their place. The technological or 'long wave' (Freeman 1984) explanations implicitly assume that the dominant innovation (here the railways) somehow absorbs so much interest and so many resources in capital and management that alternative opportunities for innovation are neglected. Now it has to be noted that the dominant innovation, the railroad, implied an outstanding development of capital market and organisation, leading to the megacorporation (Chandler 1977) in the 1880s. These were by far the largest business organisations then existing, oligopolistic organisations designed to protect the industry's profit against ruinous competition. In fact, the railway was as much or more of an innovation in the field of organisation and finance as in technology.

In my book I spoke of a redistribution of the profits of industry in favour of the oligopolistic sector ('maldistribution of profits'). In the case of the railroads we seem to note rather a redistribution of capital market funds, credits, management talent; the bankers who sat on the boards of the railway corporations must have been heavily biased in favour of the megacorporation and against financing innovations in new fields and new enterprises.

The crisis of the railroads manifested itself in 1894–98 as a consequence of a recession which we may suspect to have resulted from a general shift to the oligopoly sector at the expense of consumption. Thus behind the argument of the dominant industry and its role in the decline there are again the more complicated effects of oligopoly in the field of organisation.

Let me briefly touch on the central ideas of my book. My concept of competition is near to the classical view. Competition has the function of eliminating excess capacity in the long run and it does this by cutting long-run profits at a given utilisation of capacity (or Kalecki's 'mark up'). Restoration of a normal degree of utilisation and a normal profit margin thus go hand in hand. Normal profit margins in this context are determined by the requirements of accumulation, i.e. what is necessary to finance investment. Accumulation is simply assumed to be somehow given by the preceding long-term development of the economy and by exogenous influences.

I insert here a very simple piece of algebra to clarify the ideas. Let us consider a closed private economy, a two-class model of an economy in which workers do not save. Let us define a vector q of the quantities of the various goods produced (only final products are considered); the economy is assumed to be vertically integrated so that there are no intermediate products and costs consist only of wages and salaries. In the following equations Y = gross national product or income and W = the wage and salary bill.

$$Y = \beta' q \tag{1}$$

$$W = \gamma' q + w'_0 1 \tag{2}$$

β, the price of the products, and γ, the marginal wage and salary cost per unit produced, are vectors. The income Y and the wage bill W are given by the inner product of the vectors and are therefore scalar. 1 is the unit vector and w_0 is the fixed wage and salary cost. The dash indicates a row vector.

At the break-even point, q_0, income equals wage and salary cost; we therefore have

$$\beta' q_0 = \gamma' q_0 + w_0' 1 \tag{3}$$

From this it follows that

$$(\beta - \gamma)' q_0 = w_0' 1 \tag{4}$$

The difference between equations (1) and (2), taking account of (4), will give profits (a scalar):

$$P = Y - W = (\beta - \gamma)' (q - q_0) \tag{5}$$

We now make use of Kalecki's profit equation,

$$P = I + C$$

where I is gross investment and C the consumption of the capitalists which we assume, for simplicity, to be independent of profits. We find then that

$$(\beta - \gamma)' (q - q_0) = I + C \tag{6}$$

If the cost–price relations are given this represents something like a multiplier equation: the outlay of the capitalists (their consumption and investment) determines the level of activity, given by the qs. The distribution of this activity between the various industries is here left open; it will depend on the structure of demand.

We now introduce the diagonal matrix q^* which represents the output capacity of the various industries, and the vector u ($u \leqq 1$), which represents utilisation of capacity ($q \leqq q^*$).
We use the following definitions

$$q^* u = q \tag{7}$$

$$q^* u_0 = q_0 \tag{8}$$

and have therefore

$$q^* (u - u_0) = q - q_0 \tag{9}$$

We now substitute this expression into equation (6):

$$(\beta - \gamma)' q^* (u - u_0) = I + C \tag{10}$$

Let us now divide both sides of this equation by $\beta' q^* = Y^*$, the capacity of the total economy in terms of money value. The lefthand side of (10) can be written

$$(1 - \frac{\gamma}{\beta})' \beta q^* \ (u - u_0)$$

where both β and q^* are diagonal matrices.

We shall now replace $\beta q^*/Y^*$ by y^*, the share of the various products' capacity in the total capacity of the economy. Equation (10), after division by Y^*, now becomes:

$$(1 - \frac{\gamma}{\beta})' y^* \ (u - u_0) = \frac{I + C}{Y^*} \tag{11}$$

Here y^* as well as q^* are diagonal matrices.

This is again a kind of multiplier equation, with some adaptations which make it more suitable for discussing long-term problems. The capacity Y^* may be taken to move in constant proportion to the value of capital — this is Harrod's case of neutral technical progress — and if we further assume that capitalists' consumption in relation to their capital remains constant then the righthand side of (11) can be regarded as a kind of index of capital accumulation: it will rise or fall when the growth rate of capital rises or falls.

The implicit multiplier is determined by the distribution parameter $(1 - \gamma/\beta)$ which takes the place of the marginal propensity to save in the ordinary multiplier analysis; it is the ratio of profit to price — the gross profit margin, weighted by the capacity in the various lines of production. If the distribution parameter is given, the speed of accumulation will determine the level of utilisation in excess of the break-even point. The distribution of utilisation over the various industries is, however, left open: this will depend on the structure of effective demand. This, it is true, depends on the distribution of income. To be realistic we should therefore have to introduce the dependence of consumption on income, just as we should also have to introduce the input–output structure of the economy (for a technical treatment see Miyazawa 1976). For the purpose of the present argument, however, this is hardly necessary and would only burden the presentation. Let us therefore assume here that the proportions of the demand for consumption goods are given and constant. The use of vectors is nevertheless justified by the wish to bypass in principle the problems of deflating macro-economic variables.

Equation (11) says nothing about how the growth rate $I + C/Y^*$ is determined. We may imagine that as a trend value it is determined by the rate of innovation and by a kind of self-perpetuating force of the long-run growth in the past. The purpose of equation (11) is to illustrate the role which distribution parameters play in the process of growth. If some of the gross profit margins (mark-ups) increase, given the growth rate of capital, then some of the utilisation rates will have to decrease in relation to the break-even point. But the break-even point itself will also have to decrease unless the increase in profit margins is only a compensation for a rise in fixed costs as a proportion of total capacity income. This can be shown by reference to equations (4) and (8):

$$(1 - \frac{\gamma}{\beta})' \beta\, q^*\, u_0 = w_0' 1$$

$$(1 - \frac{\gamma}{\beta})'\, y^*\, u_0 = \frac{w_0' 1}{Y^*} \tag{12}$$

where y^*, β and q^* are diagonal matrices.

Thus, as long as the increase in gross profit margins weighted by the industry's share in total capacity is not merely due to a shifting of fixed cost as a ratio of total capacity income to the price of the product, it will have to lead to decreases in some or all of the utilisation rates u, given the capital accumulation and the capitalists' consumption as a proportion of total capacity income.[1] Again, should capital accumulation decline, given the gross profit margin and the fixed cost in relation to capacity, some utilisation rates will have to fall. This is the usual adjustment to be expected during a recession. If low utilisation rates persist over a longer period there may be an alternative adjustment — the reduction of gross profit margins forced by new entries and intensified competition which may then restore the former rate of average utilisation.

The restoration of a normal u may come about by an increase in effective demand — by a shift to wages which is the same as a shift to consumption — or else it may come about by a reduction in

1. For a discussion of the relation of fixed costs and profit margin see Steindl 1987.

productive capacity. In the former case there will be an increase in the multiplier: the reduction in the growth rate will thus imply a structural change in favour of consumption at the cost of investment. The alternative form of adjustment, the elimination of capacity, will to some extent be inevitable if we assume that firms have very different costs and that some are at the margin of existence and profitability. They will be pushed out mostly on account of very high break-even points. The solution by way of capacity elimination will also be inevitable if there are special structural problems owing to technical change. But the expansion of demand can in principle also play a role in the re-establishment of normal capacity. In my book I relied only on the reduction in capacity because I started from a microeconomic analysis of a single industry.

Now my message was, of course, that this adjustment to a reduction in growth does not work in our modern economy and has not worked for a long time, because cut-throat competition among giant firms is exceedingly dangerous and costly. The elimination of excess capacity by competition does not work. In consequence a downward cumulative process occurs because the reduction in utilisation adversely affects investment. In this way a continuing decline of accumulation can be explained. If it stretches over many decades we may, however, well ask how it could take so long: we would have expected it to proceed rather quickly. It would seem, intuitively, that there must have been counteracting forces acting against the decline. What factor could have played this role in the case of the decline of accumulation in America? My answer was: the development of the capital market. The rise of the corporate system was bound up with a development of capital market, a broadening of this market which led to a cheapening of the sources of outside finance. The yield of shares declined in the course of time and reached a very low level in the 1920s. Issues simultaneously reached a peak. The effect must have been equivalent to a large reduction in the long-term rate of interest. It was a force counteracting the secular decline and explains the prosperity of the 1920s and the suddenness of the collapse in 1929.

The Time of Economic Miracles

The post-war decades were a surprise not only for Marxists and

Keynesians; in their earlier stages they were hailed as miracles in various countries. In dealing with the post-war period I am going to extend the discussion from the USA to the wider field of industrial countries, especially Europe. They all to a greater or lesser extent shared the experience of the pre-war crisis and unemployment and they all enjoyed rather exceptional growth of output, productivity and employment in the post-war period.

I want to carry out my explanation in two steps: I shall first explain how the high level of employment and growth initially came about. I shall then show that after these favourable conditions had been established they themselves created the forces capable of perpetuating high growth.

Taking the USA first, there was a basic stimulus from public spending which had greatly expanded in comparison with the pre-war situation. The effect of this was an expansion of effective demand even though there were no deficits. The spending (much of it military) was in part financed by taxes on corporate profits (see my paper in the *Cambridge Journal* 1979).

The result of the combination of spending and taxes on strong savers is an expansion of output by higher utilisation of capacity (90 per cent in the 1950s) up to the point at which the profits and savings remaining after the higher taxes have been paid are as great as they were before. While the profit situation of the corporations was thus not made worse by the higher taxes, the utilisation of capacity was increased and that stimulated private investment which proceeded at very high levels. To this was added the built-in stabilisation of the social security system which to some extent smoothed out fluctuations. In spite of this the fluctuations were still quite marked in USA as compared with Europe and were apparently connected with the changes in public (especially military) spending, which illustrates the importance which this spending had in the promotion of effective demand.

A subsidiary factor in the intense investment activity in the earlier period was probably the fact that corporations had only a small degree of indebtedness after the war, so that there was a large margin up to the establishment of conventional debt ratios. The banks in their turn had a wide margin of possible increase in lending. Given sufficient investment opportunities and optimism this would facilitate strong investment activity.

This optimism was indeed there. The belief in consumption as a condition and even as a guarantee of prosperity had become an important element of American capitalism, an economic religion almost as strong as the traditional protestant ethic. In view of its implications for wage policy this involved also a certain spirit of social consensus — in spite of all the qualifications which you might have to make here; the contrast with the present era is striking.

The buoyancy was also increased by the opening and expansion of foreign markets for American products which made it possible for oligopolies to escape the claustrophobic conditions of a restricted home market. The newly acquired habit of business concerns of spreading out into the most varied fields of activities also created new opportunities for investment.

In Europe public and military spending was also of great importance in some countries in expanding demand but there was, on the continent at least, an additional factor which directly stimulated private investment. Europe had, for one reason or another, been out of touch with the technological development in the USA and so a backlog of innovative opportunities had accumulated which, after the war, became available in one tranche, facilitated by Marshall plan and technical assistance. Europe was catching up technologically with the USA, which meant that it was going through a technical evolution, which had taken much longer to develop originally,with great rapidity. Productivity growth at that time was roughly twice as high in Europe as in the USA. It stands to reason that this provided a very strong stimulus to investment activity. On the supply side the barriers to exceptionally fast growth were removed by the availability of labour from agriculture (in West Germany by displaced persons).

Thus an exceptional speed of development was made possible by drawing on reserves of knowhow and of labour. This process must have been exhausted long before the end of the prosperity phase in the 1970s, but in the meantime an automatic buoyancy had developed in both Europe and in USA.

The usual danger into which an accumulation process would run, that of creating overcapacity and saturated demand, was somehow avoided even though we can perceive that the intensity of the process weakened; in the USA this can be seen from the declining utilisation rates (from 90 per cent in the 1950s to 80 per cent in 1969–73). In European countries the weakening of the process could be seen in cruder signs. In Italy it made itself felt very early, in West

Germany it was acutely felt in the second half of the 1960s. But in spite of all this no major setback, no change in the general climate of confidence, occurred until the 1970s. This was due to two major elements which were in strong contrast to pre-war circumstances: the labour market and foreign trade.

The high (in Europe: full) employment increased the bargaining powers of the workers and the unions. Large concerns were very interested in maintaining a stable efficient and satisfied labour force and were therefore willing to share the extra profits arising from increased productivity with the workers. The workers pressed their demands wherever they felt that profits had increased. Workers' share of additional returns due to technological advance or to favourable market conditions was thus secured. However much the working of oligopolistic conditions might prevent competition from bringing down prices in alignment with the reduced cost of production, the pressure of wages made a shift of income to profits unlikely.

With a certain stability of the share of labour in the income being to some extent assured, the chances of finding markets for the new goods, the television sets, the washing machines and the cars were good. The philosophy of consumption and high wages worked. (A less desirable consequence was the great differentiation of wage levels in different sectors of the economy.)

The other element which kept profit margins within limits was international competition. Here again the conditions were completely different from those of the pre-war period because of liberalisation and GATT agreements, the multinationals and intense technological competition. A further important condition for the continuation of growth was the relative absence of the foreign balance constraint (if we except Britain where this constraint played a major role). The scarcity of dollars in the first post-war period had been taken care of by the Marshall plan and US loans, a direct and indirect supply of dollars, while within Europe the European payments union helped. No doubt there was still plenty of disturbance but it was not enough to reverse the growth trend. Cooperation in the international field prevailed, because Western democracy felt the obligation of making a good show in comparison with the East. This motivation was very clear in the competitive efforts in the field of education and research.

The Great Disarray

Surprising as the preceding prosperity had appeared the change of events in the 1970s was even less expected and caused a great deal of disorientation among forecasters. As I have already said, I do not think that my original maturity explanation of the previous stagnation could be applied at all directly to the new development. The reasons stem from what I have just said about the conditions of the labour market and about international competition, both of which would make it unlikely that oligopolies would have been able to increase their mark up in the period of high employment (the situation was different in the later period of unemployment, especially in the crisis of the 1980s).

There is, however, an alternative version of my stagnation theory which is also mentioned in my book. It says that oligopolistic concerns, knowing as they do that excess capacity in their market is very difficult to remove and constitutes a major embarrassment, will be much more reluctant to expand capacity than firms under competitive conditions. This consideration would still apply in post-war conditions, when considerable concentration of industry had been taking place, even though, as already said, the oligopolistic claustrophobia was somewhat lessened by the possibility of extending production by direct investment in other countries.

I am now inclined, however, to extend my reasoning even further in this direction. The development and persistence of oligopolistic market structures over a long time cannot have been without effect on the internal structure, organisation and management of firms. This partly concerns size and its consequences and partly it is a matter of the aims and preoccupations of management. From being concerned with production and sales their interest has shifted more and more to concern with market power and domination. Large firms are bureaucratic and hierarchically organised. This has been a handicap for research and development because projects have to run through committees and become the object of departmental rivalries. Large concerns have been losing research personnel to smaller firms because research workers dislike hierarchies and bureaucracy. It has been one of the lasting effects of the high employment period that the human factor has gained more weight in industry. Large concerns are invariably accused of inflexibility (see, for example, the shift to smaller cars in USA). The types of manager which came to dominate in these concerns in the USA in the post-war decades have been described as bureaucratic and adjusted to dealing with 'big government' and large unions (*Business Week*: 'The new corporate elite', January 1985).

The interest in market dominance and power which is mainly operated by mergers and take-overs has led to a shift from production to finance (from a production point of view the mergers are rarely a success, in the view of experienced managers). Some large concerns (you can easily think of examples in Britian or West Germany) derive a great part of their profits from financial and real estate business. Financial investment has played an increasing role by comparison with real investment. More recently the monetarist policy of Britain and the USA has reinforced the tendency of industrial firms to convert themselves into rentiers and speculators.

These structural changes in the organisation of business are capable of explaining a weakening of the incentive to invest. Maturity, in this perspective, has taken on a new shape in so far as it has affected the internal organisation of the concerns and the character and strategy of their managers. While the degeneration described has been proceeding gradually through the years, the change in economic climate which was telescoped into a few years was precipitated by a number of events.

The most important was the breakdown of economic international cooperation. The first clear signal of this occurred when the USA went off the gold standard and exchange rates were given free rein two years later. This created an expectation or fear of inflation and led to violent speculation in gold and commodities (Kaldor 1983, p. 32). It finally culminated in the first oil shock. To a very large extent world inflation was the consequence of this disarray. Exchange rates have been chaotic ever since, dominated by capital movements rather than price or cost relations. The fact that in all those years there was not a single really serious attempt to get substantial agreement between the major powers on the questions of exchange rates, interest rates, capital movements, debts and, last but not least, world-wide mass unemployment, is a proof of my contention that international cooperation in the West has broken down. It also illustrates the fundamental change in attitudes toward unemployment. The reason for this change can be found in a reaction against the welfare state and increasing taxation.

It may be admitted, however, that this major change in outlook was also influenced by the fact that full-employment policies were bound to be more difficult than before. In USA especially (where, however, full employment was never adhered to consistently) there was a strong increase in the growth rate of labour supply in the 1970s. A full-employment policy would therefore have required increasing the rate of growth of GDP of something of the order of 1 per cent. At the same time a series of factors emerged which were likely to create unusual uncertainties. There was the environmental problem which had received official recognition in 1969 and which obviously affected investment decisions and plans, presumably unfavourably. The same was true for the changed energy situation. There was, moreover, increased uncertainty with respect to the way technological development would go, not only in connection with energy use but also in raw materials, electronics, etc. The superiority of large-scale production, a seemingly cast iron rule of economics as well as practical management, had been put in doubt, for technological as well as organisational reasons.

This undermining of major principles was likely to create uncertainty. Smoke-stack industry was already in crisis and saturation occurred in various fields. There was equal uncertainty about the way consumption was likely to develop. How would further increases in income be spent? This is a field for innovation like others and therefore full of risks and hesitations. (The young people of the preceding decade had created certain patterns, but this movement seems to have become less vigorous. It showed, however, that consumption, too, is a pioneering affair.)

It was these kind of difficulties which bureaucratic firms and the politicians were ill prepared to face. This is true for the USA as well as for Europe. The optimist may have been inclined to say that the structural crisis will force people to learn and to devise better forms of organisation. Unfortunately what has happened in the last years does not look like learning. Young people certainly do not learn industrial skills on the streets and politicians seem to have spent these years forgetting whatever they knew before.

References

Business Week, 'The new corporate elite', 21 January 1985.
Chandler, A.D. (1977) *The Visible Hand*, Harvard University Press.

Freeman, C. (ed.) (1984) *Long Waves in the World Economy*, Francis Pinter.

Hansen, A.H. (1938) *Full Recovery or Stagnation?*, W.W. Norton.

Kaldor, N. (1983) 'The role of commodity prices in economic recovery', *Lloyds Bank Review*, July.

Kalecki, M. (1954) *Theory of Economic Dynamics*, Allen and Unwin.

Kuznets, S. (1961) *Capital in the American Economy*, NBER.

Miyazawa, K. (1976) *Input-output Analysis and the Structure of Income Distribution*, Springer Verlag.

Morishima, M. (1984) *The Economics of Industrial Society*, Cambridge University Press.

Rothbarth, E. (1946) 'Causes of the superior efficiency of USA industry as compared with British industry', *Economic Journal*, vol. 56, no. 223.

Steindl, J. (1952) *Maturity and Stagnation in the American Economy*, Oxford University Press.

Steindl, J. (1979) 'Stagnation theory and stagnation policy', *Cambridge Journal of Economics*, vol. 3, no. 1.

Steindl, J. (1987) 'Kalecki's theory of pricing: notes on the margin', in G. Fink, G. Pöll and M. Riese (eds), *Economic Theory, Political Power and Social Justice: Festschrift Kasimierz Laski*, Springer-Verlag.

6

J.A. Schumpeter

TOM BOTTOMORE

In 1981 a volume of essays published under the title *Schumpeter's Vision* (Heertje 1981) reassessed, forty years on, the arguments and predictions expounded in Schumpeter's best-known book, *Capitalism, Socialism and Democracy*. These essays marked, in a particularly striking way, the notable revival of interest in Schumpeter's work that has taken place in the past two decades over a very wide area of the social sciences; among sociologists and political scientists as well as economists, and among conservative, liberal and Marxist thinkers.

How are we to account for this reawakening of interest in a social scientist whose major innovative writings were published between 1912 and 1942, who established no school and who never became a public figure? The answer, I think, is that the issues upon which his analysis focused are precisely those which engage us again in the late twentieth century, at the end of the post-war boom; and that his approach to these issues, which is broadly historical and sociological, now evokes a stronger response, in an intellectual climate formed partly by the resurgence of Marxist economics, which seems to favour the development of a new 'political economy'.

In this essay I shall try to show, 'in desperate brevity', as Schumpeter himself was fond of saying, the nature of his distinctive ideas and their development, particularly in relation to Marxist thought, which was for him, as for Max Weber, the theoretical system that he most desired to contest and to rival.

Schumpeter was born in 1883 into a middle class family, his father a textile manufacturer in Triesch, Moravia, his mother the daughter of a doctor in Wiener-Neustadt. When Schumpeter was four years old his father died and in 1893 his mother married again, her second husband being an army general who occupied a position of both social and military importance as the commander of the Vienna garrison. Schumpeter grew up in an aristocratic milieu, attended an exclusive school for the sons of the aristocracy, the Theresianum, and was profoundly affected by this experience; as his later Harvard colleagues remarked in their memorial volume, 'he remained to the end the cultivated Austrian gentleman of the old school who had seen everything but who found in the succession of events from 1914 onward no very striking evidence of progress' (Harris 1951).

This disenchantment, or at least a somewhat detached and sceptical view of the civilisation of industrial capitalism, can perhaps be discerned in some of his later writings; but it is not the main source of his distinctive vision of the modern world. On the other hand, the contrast between his middle class origins and his aristocratic upbringing may have been important in forming his character. Smithies, in the memorial volume I have mentioned, suggests that:

> It is difficult for a young boy to be neutral to such a situation. He is either overwhelmed by it or sets out to master it. Schumpeter was of the latter sort. He adopted the manners, the habits, and the tastes of the aristocrat. I think the Theresianum had much to do with instilling in him the passion for perfection and the spirit of intellectual independence that were so prominent throughout his whole life. But he must have realized that conspicuous success in the normal aristocratic pursuits — the diplomatic service or the army — was unlikely, and, besides, they would not afford him the intellectual life he demanded. To be anything less than first-class in his chosen line of endeavour would have been unthinkable to him. He therefore had to strike out on a line of his own.

This he did during his years as a student of law and economics at the University of Vienna from 1901 to 1906 and it is to those years that we must turn to discover the real germination of his economic and social ideas. Schumpeter devoted most of his attention to economics (although after graduation he practised as a lawyer for two years in Cairo) and in particular he attended the seminars of

Wieser and Böhm-Bawerk, the latter being memorable for debates with two young Marxist thinkers, Otto Bauer and Rudolf Hilferding, who were leading figures in the nascent school of Austro–Marxism.

There were three main direct influences on Schumpeter's intellectual development in this period. The first was that of the Austrian marginalist school represented by Menger, Wieser and Böhm-Bawerk and of the closely related school of Lausanne. Schumpeter greatly admired, in particular, Walras's equilibrium system and as we shall see he also admired aspects of the work of Walras's successor in Lausanne, Pareto. Second, there was the particular influence of Wieser, who was a historian and sociologist as well as an economist; and as Schumpeter (1951a) wrote in his obituary notice,

> the chief work of Wieser's later years, however, centred in sociology, in the sense in which it may be defined as an analysis of history, or, as he himself defined it with that power he had of coining striking words, as 'history without names'. Historical Sociology, or Sociological History, had been his first interest, and it was to be his last.

Schumpeter's own orientation towards history and sociology can only have been strengthened by the third major influence on his thought, that of Marxist theory.

The importance which Schumpeter attached to historical studies especially is shown very clearly in his discussion of the nature of economic analysis in his last book, the *History of Economic Analysis*. There he says (Chapter 2, pp. 12–13):

> What distinguishes the 'scientific' economist from all the other people who think, talk, and write about economic topics is a command of techniques that we class under three heads: history, statistics, and 'theory.' The three together make up what we shall call Economic Analysis. [Later in this chapter, J.A.S. added to these three a fourth fundamental field, Economic Sociology, dealing with the 'general forms of human behaviour'.] ... Of these fundamental fields, economic history — which issues into and includes present-day facts — is by far the most important. I wish to state right now that if, starting my work in economics afresh, I were told that I could study only one of the three but could have my choice, it would be economic history that I should choose. And this on three grounds. First, the subject matter of eco-

> nomics is essentially a unique process in historic time. Nobody can hope to understand the economic phenomena of any, including the present, epoch who has not an adequate command of historical *facts* and an adequate amount of historical *sense* or of what may be described as *historical experience*. Second, the historical report cannot be purely economic but must inevitably reflect also 'institutional' facts that are not purely economic: therefore it affords the best method for understanding how economic and non-economic facts *are* related to one another and how the various social sciences *should* be related to one another. Third, it is, I believe, the fact that most of the fundamental errors currently committed in economic analysis are due to the lack of historical experience more often than to any other shortcoming of the economist's equipment. History must of course be understood to include fields that have acquired different names as a consequence of specialization, such as pre-historic reports and ethnology (anthropology).

In fact Schumpeter did choose to concentrate on the historical aspect in all his work, whether he was tracing the development of economic doctrines or analysing the dynamics of capitalism.

But we should also not overlook the more diffuse, stimulating influence of the remarkable intellectual efflorescence that characterised Vienna in the period from the 1890s to 1914; and in particular the intense discussion of the methods of the social sciences provoked by neo-Kantian and positivist philosophies of science. Schumpeter, like the Austrian marginalists and the Austro–Marxists (and unlike most Anglo–Saxon economists), was profoundly interested in problems of method. His first book, *The Nature and Main Contents of Theoretical Economics* (1908) dealt with such questions, and it was followed in 1914 by the much better known *Economic Doctrine and Method* (English translation 1954). In much of his later writing — notably in *Capitalism, Socialism and Democracy* and in the *History of Economic Analysis* — he returned to the subject, elucidating, analysing and criticising the approaches of other economists and sociologists, while expressing his own methodological views largely in an indirect way and by implication, rather than in the form of a systematic exposition. I do not intend to pursue these methodological issues at any great length here, but simply draw attention to an ambiguity, even contradiction, in Schumpeter's somewhat eclectic approach which is relevant to my main theme and reflects the influence upon his work of two important currents of thought that I have already mentioned: Austrian marginal utility theory and Austro–Marxism.

On one hand Schumpeter adopted the 'subjectivist' standpoint of the Austrian school (his assessment of which is most clearly set out in the essays on Menger and Böhm-Bawerk in *Ten Great Economists*); and he was committed, from this standpoint, to an analysis of economic phenomena in terms of the actions, resulting from subjective valuations, of individuals. Indeed he seems to have coined (in his book of 1908) the term 'methodological individualism', the use of which was later extended from the purely economic to the social field by Popper and others.

On the other hand, Schumpeter acquired from Marxism a view of the economic and social process in which 'impersonal' forces bring about major structural changes. Thus in his preface to the Japanese edition of the *Theory of Economic Development*, after noting that his aim in that book is to present 'a purely economic theory of economic change', he continues:

> It was not clear to me at the outset what to the reader will perhaps be obvious at once, namely, that this idea and this aim are exactly the the same as the idea and the aim which underlie the economic teaching of Karl Marx. In fact, what distinguishes him from the economists of his own time and those who preceded him, was precisely a vision of economic evolution as a distinct process generated by the economic system itself... It is probably due to this fact that one generation of economists after another turns back to him again, although they may find plenty to criticize in him.

And again, later, in the *History of Economic Analysis* Schumpeter observed that Marx, for whom development was the 'central theme ... concentrated his analytic powers on the task of showing how the economic process, changing itself by virtue of its own inherent logic, is incessantly changing the social framework — the whole of society in fact'.

In all of this there is little or no reference to the 'subjective valuations' of individuals, and in a great deal of Schumpeter's substantive economic analysis we are confronted with a kind of determinism resembling the more extreme structuralist conceptions of the 1960s in which economic and social structures, through their own logic, generate their temporal successors. This is true, for example, of his account of the 'socialisation' of the economy (a notion derived from Marx), and of his initial statement (afterwards heavily qualified, however) of the thesis expounded in *Capitalism, Socialism and Democracy*: that 'a socialist form of society will inevitably emerge from an equally inevitable decomposition of capitalist society'.

I do not think Schumpeter ever resolved, or even set out to resolve in a systematic way, the inconsistencies or contradictions posed by these two different methods. Sometimes he seemed to suggest that the methods were appropriate to different problems; for example, those of equilibrium or of development. Thus in his essay on Menger (1951a) he says, 'To avoid misunderstanding: no economic sociology or sociology of economic development can be derived from Menger's work. It makes only a small contribution to the picture of economic history and the struggle of social classes, but Menger's theory of value, price and distribution is the best we have up to now'. Yet in his earlier essay on Böhm-Bawerk he said of the latter's critical monograph on Marx (provoked by the publication of the third volume of *Capital*) that 'it will never cease to be *the* critique of Marx in so far as the theoretical content of Marx's system is concerned', but then concluded 'I cannot, however, consider it in further detail'.

It is a great pity, in terms of a clarification of his own method, that Schumpeter did not do so, and especially that he did not discuss the response to Böhm-Bawerk, embodying a general criticism of subjective value theory, published by Hilferding (1904). Even in his last years Schumpeter, while bestowing high praise on the Austro-Marxist thinkers in a brief passage in the *History of Economic Analysis*, again sidestepped the issue by saying that 'Hilferding ... wrote a notable reply to Böhm-Bawerk's criticism of Marx ... and other things, which a fuller review could not pass by ...'

The vagaries of Schumpeter's methodological views have never, so far as I know, been subjected to a thorough critical scrutiny, although one contributor to the memorial volume published in 1951 discussed briefly what he called Schumpeter's 'methodological tolerance'. The eclecticism is, however, very evident in the introduction to the *History of Economic Analysis*, in the passage I have cited, where Schumpeter distinguishes the four techniques (understood in a broad sense as methodological approaches), of history, statistics, theory and economic sociology, without attempting to show how, or whether, they are separated, connected, autonomous or interdependent.

These methodological weaknesses and inconsistencies reveal themselves, and have their effects, in two spheres of Schumpeter's work on which I propose to concentrate here: his theory of social classes, and his analysis of the (probable) transition from capitalism to socialism. The essay on classes, originating in lectures given in 1910, was published in 1927 but was then largely ignored until an English translation (together with a translation of an equally neglected essay on imperialism) was published in 1951, edited and introduced by Paul Sweezy (1951b). In this essay Schumpeter first sets out very clearly the range of problems with which a theory of classes has to deal and then concentrates upon one of these problems — the formation of classes — which he proceeds to analyse in terms of the rise and fall of whole classes. The context of his study is quite evidently the Marxist theory of class, which provides much of the framework of his analysis, but he diverges from the Marxist view — which indeed it was his purpose to criticise — in several important respects. First, he dismisses the idea of an original 'classless situation' in human society (except possibly in isolated cases). Second, he introduces into his account of the formation of classes an individual, subjective element (pp. 154–155):

> A first reason for shifting family position is offered by the automatism of accumulation, asserted by Marx. The 'capitalist' who is bigger at the outset of the period captures more profit than the smaller one. His proportionate accumulation is therefore larger, and he improves his productive plant more rapidly. The discrepancy grows, until the wealthier exploiter outstrips the poorer one in the competitive field and forces him to the wall. This view is a typical example of how bias in favour of a theory blinds the theorist to the simplest facts, grotesquely distorting their proportions. Manifestly, the captured surplus value *does not invest itself* but must *be invested*. This means on the one hand that it must not be consumed by the capitalist, and on the other hand that the important point is *how* it is invested. Both factors lead away from the idea of objective automatism to the field of behaviour and motive — in other words, from the *social* 'force' to the *individual* — physical or family; from the *objective* to the *subjective*. It may be objected that the logic of the social situation forces the individual to invest his profits, that individual motivation is only a fleeting intermediate phase.

> This is true, as far as it goes, and must be acknowledged by any reasonable person. Naturally the individual psyche is no more than a product, an offshoot, a reflex, and conductor of the inner necessities of any given situation. But the crucial factor is that the social logic or objective situation does not unequivocally determine *how much* profit shall be invested, and *how* it shall be invested, *unless individual disposition is taken into account*. Yet when that is done, the logic is no longer inherent solely in the system as distinct from the individuality of the industrialist himself. Marx, in fact, in this case as in general, implies an assumption about average behaviour — an assumption that includes an economic psychology, however imperfect.

And Schumpeter emphasises, later in the essay, as being of major importance for rising into a higher class, 'the method of striking out along unconventional paths'. Most industrial families, he says, have risen 'because one of their members has *done something novel*, typically the founding of a new enterprise'. Clearly this view is bound up with his conception of the role of the entrepreneur in modern capitalism which he was elaborating just at the time when the lectures on class were first given.

Third, in analysing the rise and fall of whole classes Schumpeter ignores completely the factor of class conflict; that is, conflict between a dominant class and a subordinate class or classes. His argument is expressed in terms of social functions: 'the position of each class in the total national structure depends, on the one hand, on the significance that is attributed to (its) function, and, on the other hand, on the degree to which the class sucessfully performs the function'. Thus, in the rest of this part of the essay, Schumpeter traces the decline of the feudal nobility as a consequence of the loss or surrender of its function, but at the same time he turns more in this case to an 'objective' explanation, observing that this process implied 'not merely voluntary surrender and failure of will power, but also the pressure of the objective social situation' (p. 197), and again, 'Naturally our process was determined by economic developments' (p. 199).

On several points Schumpeter is much closer to a theory of the circulation of elites than to a theory of social classes and he suggests this himself in his essay on Pareto (1951a), claiming that it is to the credit of Pareto's sociology that for him 'the historical process is not so much the result of the conflict of comprehensive social classes as it is the result of the conflict of their ruling minorities', adding that 'property relations *per se* are much less in evidence with Pareto than they are with Marx' and that 'this also constitutes a claim to superiority of the Paretian analysis'.

One last feature of Schumpeter's study of the rise and fall of whole classes deserves attention; namely, that it concentrates wholly on the *fall*. The decline of the nobility through loss of its function is briefly charted, but the rise of the 'new class' is not discussed at all. And in the *Theory of Economic Development* where Schumpeter first set out his distinctive view of the role of the entrepreneur as a new social type who is the 'fundamental phenomenon' of capitalist development, he deliberately put aside the question of the historical origins of the entrepreneur, stating flatly that 'no historical evolutionary factors will be indicated ... like changes in the mentality of economic men ... and so forth'.

It is illuminating to consider, in relation to the essay on social classes, Schumpeter's subsequent analysis of the decline of capitalism. In *Capitalism, Socialism and Democracy* he makes no direct reference at all to his own study of classes, though he devotes some pages to criticising Marx's conception; nevertheless, it is at once apparent that the pattern of analysis is identical with that adopted in his essay. Once again he traces the decline of one class without paying any attention to the rise of another or examining the actual course of this social transformation. The social function of the entrepreneur, he argues, is disappearing with the growth of the modern corporation, as 'economic progress tends to become depersonalized and automatized (and) bureau and committee work tends to replace individual action', and he continues:

> This affects the position of the entire bourgeois stratum ... Economically and sociologically, directly and indirectly, the bourgeoisie ... depends on the entrepreneur and, as a class, lives and will die with him ... The perfectly bureaucratized giant industrial unit not only ousts the small or medium-sized firm and 'expropriates' its owners, but in the end it also ousts the entrepreneur and expropriates the bourgeoisie as a class.

This process of eliminating the entrepreneur, and hence the whole bourgeoisie, is given a further impetus, according to Schumpeter, by the increasing intervention of the state in economic life.

But what is it that animates this whole process, leading in Schumpeter's view to socialism? It is not any identifiable class: the intellectuals are critics of capitalism, helping to undermine it, but they are not a class seeking power (as some other social theorists have conceived them); bureaucratisation is an important feature of the process that Schumpeter describes, but bureaucrats likewise are not conceived as a new 'dominant class'. More generally, Schumpeter insisted that 'socialism ... in reality has nothing to do with the presence or absence of social classes'. This, of course, is nonsense. The whole socialist movement, historically considered, is a class movement and its ultimate goal has been, and remains (in however attenuated a form), the creation of a 'classless society'. In what sense, and to what degree, that goal is achievable, is another question.

Schumpeter's own theory of the advent of socialism is quite different from that of socialists, especially Marxist socialists, themselves. It is narrowly economic and very deterministic, notwithstanding the qualifications that were introduced in later editions of *Capitalism, Socialism and Democracy*. Schumpeter, dismissing any conception of socialism as involving 'a new cultural world', defined what he always referred to as 'centralist socialism' as 'that organization of society in which the means of production are controlled, and the decisions on how and what to produce and on who is to get what, are made by public authority instead of by privately-owned and privately-managed firms'. The advent of socialism, in this strictly economic sense, results from the process in which the economy 'socializes itself'; a notion which Schumpeter, with due acknowledgement, derived from Marx, and perhaps more immediately from the writings of Hilferding on 'organised capitalism'. But this concept of a gradual 'socialisation' of the economy, as Schumpeter employs it, is too broad and vague to define the advent of a specific form of society. The economic dominance of large-scale enterprises is no doubt (for both Marx and Schumpeter) a prime factor in the process whereby the economy 'socialises' itself; but another important factor is the conscious intervention of the state and, as I have argued elsewhere, different outcomes are possible — a corporate economy, a totalitarian state economy, a new type of capitalism — depending on which class, or other social group, controls the state power (Bottomore 1985, p. 77).

The principal weakness in Schumpeter's account of the transition from capitalism to socialism is, then, its excessively economistic and determinist character; and correspondingly, its neglect of the actions of individuals and groups in the political arena. From this standpoint Marx's conception, and especially the conceptions of some later Marxists, of the transition are distinctly superior, because they embrace both elements: on one side the socialisation of the economy which establishes the preconditions for socialism; on the other, the struggle of a politically organised class to bring about, in reality, a socialist form of society.

In this sense a Marxist analysis also takes more explicitly into account a fundamental characteristic of the constitution and perpetual transformation of human societies: the presence of two different kinds of possible effect, resulting either from the actions of human agents (individual or collective) or from the 'causal powers' of underlying structures of social life. This has become a dominant issue in recent methodological discussions in the social sciences, more particularly in sociology (Outhwaite 1987). Schumpeter, on the other hand, did not pay much attention to the distinction between agency and structure, but simply approached his subject matter sometimes in one way, sometimes in another. It would undoubtedly be valuable to examine his work more extensively and more rigorously in the light of recent studies in the philosophy of the social sciences and as part of a more general enquiry into the methods of the new political economy.

In a text written at the very end of his life, 'The march into socialism' (which was appended to later editions of *Capitalism, Socialism and Democracy*), Schumpeter, as I have already noted, did in fact substantially qualify the determinism of his analysis, asserting that he was not prophesying or predicting the advent of socialism, only diagnosing 'observable tendencies', and stating (p. 422):

> what the results would be, if these tendencies should work themselves out according to their logic. In itself this does not amount to prognosis or prediction because factors external to the chosen range of observation may intervene to prevent that consummation; because, with phenomena so far removed as social phenomena are from the comfortable situation that astronomers have the good fortune of facing, observable tendencies, even if allowed to work themselves out, may be compatible with more than one outcome; and because existing tendencies, battling with resistances, may fail to work themselves out completely, and may eventually 'stick' at some halfway house.

Schumpeter goes on to consider very briefly some of the alternative possible outcomes: 'some form of guild socialism' rather than 'centralist socialism', 'forms of social organization that are not socialist at all', various compromise arrangements in the case of independent farmers or small businessmen, a loss of momentum in the migration of economic affairs from the private to the public sphere as many of the urges which favour this migration become satisfied.

From one aspect these qualifications bring Schumpeter's analysis somewhat closer to a Marxist one, inasmuch as diverse political considerations are now brought into it. But they can also be interpreted as undermining parts of his preceding analysis of the transition and suggesting quite a different conception of the future, in terms of the survival of what has been called a 'plausible capitalism'. This is the view taken by some contributors to the book *Schumpeter's Vision* (Heertje 1981). They are, however, critical in the first place of Schumpeter's central thesis — the decline of the entrepreneur — and argue that the post-war development of capitalism has demonstrated, in the words of the editor, 'more room for dynamic entrepreneurial activity than Schumpeter foresaw, especially in smaller scale operations'. But this criticism seems to me misplaced, for what is at issue is not the scope for entrepreneurial activity in peripheral and secondary areas of the economy, but the nature of the dominant force in post-war economic development. Here it seems to me that Schumpeter's prognosis was quite correct; it is the growth of large corporations and massive state intervention in the economy — in short, 'organised' or 'managed' capitalism — which has been the crucial factor in economic expansion at a rate higher than in any previous period. Furthermore, the differences between countries can be related in large measure to the extent of effective public management; the continuing economic decline of Britain contrasting sharply with the economic performance of those societies which are more socialist (e.g. Sweden, Austria) or which have in other forms a higher level of state intervention in the economy (e.g. France, West Germany, Japan).

A second line of argument against Schumpeter's original predictions seems to me more persuasive. 'Organised' or 'managed' capitalism, corresponding roughly with Schumpeter's 'halfway house', can be represented as a new type of capitalism which may prove enduring, at least for the foreseeable future. Thus William Fellner concludes his essay in *Schumpeter's Vision* by saying (p. 67) that:

> If by a system we mean a set of economic and social relations that remain characteristic of a period of reasonable length, and if one places oneself in Schumpeter's world, as it was first described in his *Theory of Economic Development*, then capitalism should be expected to include a succession of systems rather than to be a single system. Whether in *Capitalism, Socialism and Democracy* Schumpeter has explained the transformation of a system in this sense into another variety of capitalism or, as he believed, a decomposition process leading into centralized socialism, is a question which his reasoning does not decide. The answer will depend on the relative strength of several currents, all of which clearly possess significance on the contemporary Western scene.

I think we can approach an answer to this question by bringing into the analysis another element in Schumpeter's conception of the development of capitalism, namely, his theory of business cycles, and in particular his emphasis on 'long waves'. Schumpeter's 'gales of creative destruction' which periodically sweep through the capitalist economy as a result of surges in technological innovation correspond broadly, in their significance and effects, with the economic crises described by Marx, although Marx confined his attention to much shorter cycles and in any case did not elaborate his theory of crises in a systematic way. The question then is, whether these crises do, as Marx sometimes suggested, 'put the existence of the entire bourgeois society on trial, each time more threateningly', or whether they are, in a more restricted sense, 'creatively destructive', constantly renewing the capitalist system in new forms.

I do not think there is any simple or definitive answer to this question; but it is at any rate arguable that after every serious crisis (in regard to which we should also take account of the effects of major wars) a further socialisation of the economy is consciously and deliberately undertaken (in the context of class politics) at a higher lever than was achieved on the preceding occasion (Bottomore 1985, pp.79–81). The contest between capitalism and socialism is far from being concluded and Schumpeter's halfway house is not necessarily a final resting place. On a world scale, though not of course in Britain, socialism has shown signs of advancing again, and I venture to predict, in Schumpeter's weaker sense and for the medium term of forty years which he considered the limit for such predictions, that the socialist economies will gradually come to exercise a much greater influence on the world economy and on world affairs more generally and thus open the way for various new forms of socialist society.

It is possible, then, to derive from Schumpeter's work (though with some limitations, arising mainly from the exclusion of class-based politics from his analysis) a conception of the transition from capitalism to socialism which has some striking affinities with a Marxist view. This affinity, in the conditions of the present economic recession, no doubt accounts in large measure for the revival of interest in his work. As T.W. Hutchison (1982) wrote in a review of *Schumpeter's Vision*:

> Joseph Schumpeter and Keynes were the two major economists of their generation. Both were born in 1883 and died shortly after the Second World War. Undoubtedly, with the 'Revolution' named after him, Keynes quite overshadowed Schumpeter in the 1940s, 50s and 60s. Now, in the 1980s, for an allegedly almost chronically crisis-ridden subject, perhaps Schumpeter's work, and his style as an economist, have more to offer.

I would put this more strongly and say that there is now a good case for regarding Schumpeter as the greatest economist of his generation, and quite certainly as one of the small number of outstanding social scientists of the twentieth century, comparable in his achievement with Max Weber. In his lifetime there was no Schumpeterian 'school'; today it seems that something resembling a 'school' or 'tendency', with various subdivisions, is vigorously alive and growing and is likely to outlast many a current fashion. Recognising this, we might well say of Schumpeter what he himself said of Marx: that 'one generation of economists after another turns back to him again, though they may find plenty to criticize in him'.

References

Bottomore, Tom (1985) *Theories of Modern Capitalism*, Allen and Unwin.
Harris, S.E. (ed.) (1951) *Schumpeter, Social Scientist*, Harvard University Press.

Heertje, Arnold (ed.) (1981) *Schumpeter's Vision*, Praeger.
Hilferding, R. (1949) *Böhm-Bawerk's Marx-Kritik*, Augustus M. Kelley, New York.
Hutchison, T.W. (1982) 'Capitalism and its prospects', *Times Literary Supplement*, 5 February.
Outhwaite, William (1987) *New Philosophies of Social Science*, Macmillan.
Schumpeter, J.A. (1908) *Das Wesen und der Hauptinhalt der theoretischen Nationalökonomie*, Duncker and Humblot, Munich and Leipzig.
Schumpeter, J.A. (1912) *The Theory of Economic Development: An Inquiry into Profits, Capital, Credit, Interest, and the Business Cycle*, Harvard University Press.
Schumpeter, J.A. (1914) *Economic Doctrine and Method*, Allen and Unwin.
Schumpeter, J.A. (1951a) *Ten Great Economists: From Marx to Keynes*, Allen and Unwin.
Schumpeter, J.A. (1951b) *Imperialism and Social Classes*, Blackwell.
Schumpeter, J.A. (1954) *History of Economic Analysis*, Allen and Unwin.
Schumpeter, J.A. (1987) *Capitalism, Socialism and Democracy*, Allen and Unwin.

7

Paul M. Sweezy

MICHAEL A. LEBOWITZ

Described by the *Wall Street Journal* as 'the "Dean" of radical economics', Paul Sweezy has more than any other single person kept Marxist economics alive in North America.[1] One work would be sufficient to have achieved this — *The Theory of Capitalist Development* (first published in 1942). During the period of the 1950s and 1960s, this was the book to which one turned to learn about Marxist economics. As Meghnad Desai testified years later (in the introduction to his own text in Marxian economics):

> There was in those days one book that students could read if they wanted to acquaint themselves with Marx's thought. *The Theory of Capitalist Development*, when all is said and done, still remains a classic introduction to Marxian economics... It was a definitive statement of a certain period about how Marx and his system were a key to the understanding of capitalism. While the book comes in for much casual criticism today, Paul Sweezy can be credited for having kept the eventual prospect of a revival of Marxian economics alive.[2]

Similarly, two German writers, Gerd Hardach and Dieter Karras, commented in 1974 that 'as an analytical and exhaustive résumé of the history of Marxist theory up to the 1930s, Sweezy's book is still without any rivals today'. Lending support to Desai's point, they noted that, on the eve of the rebirth of West German Marxism, the 1959 German edition of the book 'made available to the German reader a theoretical tradition which had been very largely produced in German-speaking areas and then subsequently effectively suppressed by fascism and the post-war restoration'.[3]

Yet *The Theory of Capitalist Development* was not just an introduction to Marxian economics and a transmission of a theoretical tradition. Sweezy also initially formulated there his general theory of capitalist stagnation. It is a theory which has been offered to explain not only the Depression conditions of its origins but also the post-war boom (the Golden Age) and the subsequent crisis of the 1970s and 1980s.

More than the author of a single text, however, Paul Sweezy has probed for answers about society and social change in many directions. His questions in relation to Maurice Dobb's *Studies in the Development of Capitalism* in 1950 triggered a major debate on the transition from feudalism to capitalism whose echoes reverberate today — just as a later exchange with Charles Bettelheim would pose critical questions about the transition to socialism. From his book on the Cuban Revolution (with associate Leo Huberman) to his emphasis on capitalism as a world system to his essays on post-revolutionary societies, Sweezy has addressed the important questions of our time; and no one could say (as he has about neoclassical economists) that he has concerned himself with 'smaller and decreasingly significant questions' with the result that there is 'a truly stupefying gap between the questions posed and the techniques employed to answer them'.[4]

For many, though, it is for his joint work with Paul Baran, *Monopoly Capital*, that he will be remembered. Begun in the mid-1950s, a time of 'full-fledged McCarthyism' when 'it was practically impossible for Marxist dialogue to exist within the US academy', the book became upon its publication in 1966 the introduction to radical economic analysis for an entire generation of university students and an important influence on the New Left of the period.[5] But Sweezy has never rested on his laurels. In *Monthly Review* (the magazine founded in 1949 by Sweezy and Huberman), he and his co-editor Harry Magdoff continue to analyse current economic developments and to explore their theoretical significance. After over a half century of Marxist scholarship, the Dean of radical economics continues to guide (and to receive graciously) younger colleagues and students.

None of this is the trajectory which could have been predicted at the time of Sweezy's birth in New York City on 10 April 1910. Sweezy's father was a banker, one of five vice-presidents of the First

National Bank (a predecessor of the Citibank), and Paul had the background appropriate to the scion of a wealthy family. He attended Phillips Exeter Academy and then went on to Harvard (as had his brother Alan before him). During his time there from 1928 to 1932, he edited the *Harvard Crimson* and was trained in the standard neoclassical economics.[6]

There was no sign here of his future path. And there certainly was no indication that this banker's son would become the object of a McCarthyite witch hunt by a New Hampshire subversive activities committee. Questioned in 1953, he was found guilty of contempt of court and sentenced to jail. While out on bail, he appealed against the charge which was ultimately overturned in 1957 by the US Supreme Court in one of the landmark decisions on McCarthyism.[7]

The year of his graduation, 1932, was a time of troubles. The period was one of stock market crash, bank failures, the onset of the Depression of the 1930s, the rise of Hitler and the First Soviet Five-Year Plan. And, as for so many others, these events represented a challenge to the education Sweezy had received. What, after all, did this have to do with the neoclassical economics that he had studied at Harvard?

Sweezy recalls arriving in London in 1932 for a graduate year at the London School of Economics with a feeling of 'confusion edged with resentment at the irrelevance of what I had spent the last four years trying to learn'. There, however, he found graduate students actively debating the issues of the day, a 'continuous state of intellectual and political ferment'; and, it was there that he first came into contact with Marxism. He returned to Harvard after that year 'a convinced but very ignorant Marxist'.[8]

Changes had begun at Harvard as well. Graduate students and younger faculty members were beginning to take an interest in Marxism. (Among those with whom Sweezy was to have many discussions about Marxism was Shigeto Tsuru, who later contributed an appendix to *The Theory of Capitalist Development* comparing the reproduction schemes of Quesnay, Marx and Keynes.)[9] Perhaps the most significant development for Sweezy, however, was that he met and became a student of Joseph Schumpeter who had joined the Harvard faculty in 1932. The atmosphere around Schumpeter was certain to stimulate a young economist: he organised informal seminars and discussion groups and attracted economists from around the world. What Sweezy received there, along with others in the 'Schumpeter circle', was encouragement and an atmosphere of intellectual clash and excitement. He was to describe this period subsequently as the most stimulating of his life.[10]

As it happens Sweezy took only one formal course from Schumpeter, a small graduate seminar of four or five people which included Oscar Lange and which Wassily Leontief attended. Yet he went on to become Schumpeter's assistant in an introductory graduate course in economic theory and a very close friend.[11] With Schumpeter on his thesis committee, he completed his doctoral dissertation in 1937 on the coal cartel during the English industrial revolution (for which he was awarded the David A. Wells Prize for best essay in economics by the Harvard Economics Department).

During this time, Sweezy worked at becoming 'a self-educated Marxist'. In this, too, Schumpeter was central. For, despite his own diametrically opposite political perspective, Schumpeter was 'a unique figure. He understood the importance of Marxism.' A contemporary of Hilferding and Austro–Marxists like Otto Bauer, he had architected his own theory of capitalism as a deliberate alternative to Marxism. Thus, 'he paid Marxism the compliment of understanding and recognizing that it was the most important intellectual trend of the time'.[12]

In 1938 Sweezy became an Instructor at Harvard, teaching a course on the economics of socialism (in which he had previously assisted). Attempting to increase the level of treatment of Marxism in the course, he proceeded to teach himself and to absorb the European (especially German) tradition in Marxist thought. The *Theory of Capitalist Development* was written over these years; it was 'started more or less as an effort in self-clarification'. Completed soon after the United States entered World War II, the book was published shortly before Sweezy went into the US Army in 1942.[13]

The Early Work

Yet *The Theory of Capitalist Development* was not Sweezy's first book or contribution. In a study undertaken in 1937 for the National Resources Committee (a New Deal agency), he demonstrated that, contrary to the Berle and Means classification of a substantial number of leading US corporations as 'management-controlled', it was possible to identify eight clearly definable 'interest groups', industrial and financial alliances among the large corporations.[14] To understand the control of corporations, Sweezy stressed the importance of a 'knowledge of the general policies of the companies and individuals involved' (p. 162). Citing the policies of the investment banking firm of J.P. Morgan and Co. and its alliance with the First National Bank of New York (his father's bank) in the first and most important of the interest groups, he proposed that not only stock ownership but also banking and underwriting relations were critical in tracing industrial and financial alliances (pp. 163, 168).

Within a few years, however, Sweezy proceeded to explain that the dominant role that had been played by the investment banker in the consolidation of the large firms had now declined. In part the result of the sharp decline in economic expansion during the Depression, an important explanation of this trend was 'the vast internal financial resources' at the disposal of existing large corporations which significantly reduced their necessity to resort to the capital market. Thus, the dominance of financial over industrial capital should be seen as a 'temporary stage' of capitalist development'.[15] It was a point subsequently underlined in his criticism of Hilferding in *The Theory of Capitalist Development*, where Sweezy stressed the growing importance of internal corporate financing and his preference for Lenin's concept of 'monopoly capital' over that of Hilferding's 'finance capital'.[16]

Monopoly was also the theme of Sweezy's thesis, published in 1938 as *Monopoly and Competition in the English Coal Trade, 1550–1850*. Using the records of the coal owners, Sweezy drew upon current theoretical developments in the theory of imperfect competition and applied the microeconomist's tools (in a manner to be discovered many years later by the New Economic History) to explain the behaviour of the owners and, in particular, the reasons for the emergence of excess capacity in the industry in the nineteenth century. A demand curve facing producers which was relatively elastic above the existing price and relatively inelastic below that price tended to generate, he argued, high profits and a relatively stable price. Under the existing cartel arrangements, his model also predicted 'growing individual plants with a *tendency* towards more growth than is warranted by the increase in demand'.[17]

What was particular to the early nineteenth-century English coal combination, however, had now become general as the result of the growth of large-scale production which generated a tendency for 'productive capacity to outrun the market'. The threat of cut-throat competition (and its implications for profits) engendered combination — but the fostering of monopoly would itself 'serve further to contract markets and outlets for investment'.[18]

The 'kinked demand curve' described (and presented complete with the discontinuity in the marginal revenue curve) in this study was subsequently to become well known and influential as the result of Sweezy's article, 'Demand under conditions of oligopoly', published in the following year.[19] Yet, the extension to current policy implications had occurred first in Sweezy's comments upon a paper by A.P. Lerner, 'The relation of wage policies and price policies', at the December 1938 meeting of the American Economics Association. There, he stressed the point subsequently made in his article: that under conditions of the kinked demand curve the only effect of an increase in wages may be reduced profits (rather than a change in the short-run equilibrium of price and output).[20]

The Theory of Capitalist Development

When Sweezy published his *Theory of Capitalist Development* he had already established a reputation as an important young scholar as the result of his essay on the oligopolistic demand curve. With this book, however, he added significantly to that reputation. The book introduced many to a tradition of Marxist scholarship hitherto inaccessible to Anglophones. To this day it is often remembered for opening up the discussion of the problem of 'transformation' from Marxian values to prices and for its consideration of the work of Ladislaus von Bortkiewicz on this question. Yet, on the Marxian questions of value theory, the falling tendency of the rate of profit and crisis theory, Sweezy's contribution was easily as important.

Sweezy is credited with having introduced into the discussion of Marx's theory of value the distinction between the 'quantitative-value problem' and the 'qualitative-value problem'. Despite the break with the English Marxist tradition of Maurice Dobb which stressed the basic continuity between the labour–cost approach of Smith, Ricardo and Marx (and, later, Sraffa), however, there has been a tendency to lump Sweezy together with Dobb as part of a single 'Anglo-American' tradition which effectively treats the Marxian and Ricardian theories as identical.[21]

That is simply incorrect. Indeed, the failure to understand Sweezy's early attempt to distance Marx's value theory from that of classical political economy left subsequent commentators unprepared for Sweezy's 1974 critique of Dobb's *Theories of Value and Distribution since Adam Smith: Ideology and Economic Theory*.[22] Criticising Dobb for making 'Marx seem much more like his predecessors and successors than he really was', Sweezy argued that the scope and depth of Marx's originality and his break with the classical tradition were lost in Dobb's account of the Ricardo–Marx–Sraffa tradition. In short, 'to speak of a Ricardo–Marx tradition can only be misleading for both bourgeois and Marxist economists'.[23]

The point, though, was not at all new: Sweezy had begun his discussion of value 32 years earlier by stressing 'the sharp break which divides his (Marx's) analysis from that of the classical school' (p. 23). The distinction between the 'qualitative-value problem' and the 'quantitative-value problem' was central. 'No longer can the economist afford to confine his attention to the quantitative relations arising from commodity production; he must also direct his attention to the character of social relations which underlie the commodity form' (p. 24).

Marx's distinction between 'abstract' labour and 'concrete' labour was at the core of the 'qualitative-value problem'. Abstract labour (or labour in general) was the labour represented in the value of the commodity; yet the critics of Marx's value theory had said 'hardly a word about abstract labor' (p. 34). The very concept of abstract labour, however, went beyond the forms of value on the surface, individual commodity prices, to consider the relations among human beings which were necessarily hidden by the commodity form; at the centre of the qualitative-value problem was the 'fetish character of commodities'.

It was a clear *although unacknowledged* break with Dobb's position. In elevating the qualitative-value problem, Sweezy cited as support 'the excellent note on value theory by Alfred Lowe, "Mr Dobb and Marx's Theory of Value"' (page 25, note). 'Alfred Lowe' was Shigeto Tsuru — to whom Sweezy acknowledged his 'greatest debt' for many discussions (p. vi). Tsuru *had* openly criticised

Dobb. He had argued that Dobb's very conception of value theory in his *Political Economy and Capitalism* (1937) 'presupposes already a method quite opposite to that of Marx'.[24] Citing Hilferding's argument in the response to Böhm-Bawerk (which Sweezy was later to make widely available), Tsuru proposed that the essence of Marx's value analysis was 'the *qualitative* statement specifying the social relation of the capitalist mode of production' (pp. 100, 102). Why, after all, had Marx underlined 'the importance of distinguishing the two-fold character of labour in the commodity production, as contrasted with Mr Dobb's vague definition of labour as "the expenditure of a given quantum of human energy"'?

Rejecting Dobb's argument that a theory of value must be quantitative in form and capable of expression in terms of 'quantitive entities in the real world', Tsuru argued that this was 'an insuperable task. For such an attempt has to involve factors both apparent and essential embracing the economic system as a whole. Society is the only accountant of socially necessary labour time' (p. 103). For Tsuru (whose honours thesis at Harvard College had explored Marx's methodology and commodity fetishism), Marx's 'insistence on the necessity of distinguishing between value and value-form' were critical; Dobb's focus on quantitative issues and distribution, on the other hand, was little different from that of classical political economy and, indeed, in some respects approached the 'pre-Marxian complacency' of Ricardo and John Stuart Mill (pp. 101, 104).

Sweezy's adoption of this distinction between qualitative and quantitative thus foreshadowed the subsequent debates over value which emerged among neo-Ricardians and Marxists in the wake of Sraffa's work. Indeed, Sweezy's discussion of the 'quantitative-value problem' also diverged significantly from the classical value tradition of embodied concrete labour in his stress upon the importance of 'demand'. Different traditions of value theory, then, were transmitted by Dobb and Sweezy, and this may help to explain why Sraffa's work subsequently had so much less of an impact among North American Marxists.

The significance attributed to 'the falling rate of profit' (FROP) was another such distinction between Sweezy and Dobb (and the classical tradition). Identifying Dobb as an author who had 'concluded that Marx meant the law of the falling tendency of the rate of profit to be the primary explanatory principle so far as crises are concerned', Sweezy rejected this conclusion on two important grounds (pp. 147–148). Firstly, emphasising Marx's consideration of 'counteracting tendencies', he questioned the theoretical foundations of the FROP tendency with respect to the assumption that the organic composition of capital *necessarily* increased more than the rate of surplus value; the formulation, he proposed, was 'not very convincing' (pp. 102–104).

As critical, however, was that Sweezy argued that Marx's view of crises and business cycles differed significantly from those of mainstream economists who assumed that 'the crisis is not the result but rather the cause of a shortage of effective demand' (p. 155). Implicit in the theory of value, he argued, was a theory of crisis which emanated from the inability of capitalists to sell commodities at their value (p. 146). And, at the root of such crises was the contradiction between the production of use values and the goal of producing surplus value, the fundamental contradiction of capitalism (p. 172).

This alternative explanation Sweezy labelled an 'under-consumption' theory of capitalist crises, and he proceeded to show its undeniable presence in Marx's texts. Yet, there was a critical gap — the theory had never been fully developed by Marx, and subsequent Marxists (like Rosa Luxemburg) who had turned their attention to the question had not succeeded in constructing a logical and detailed theory. The result was that 'the outstanding present-day English Marxist economist, Maurice Dobb, assigns a role to underconsumption which is distinctly secondary to that of the falling tendency of the rate of profit' (p. 179).

Completed, however, the underconsumption theory 'would have been of primary importance in the overall picture of the capitalist economy' (p. 178). To supplement Marx's work by carefully formulating the Marxian underconsumption theory, then, was the project Sweezy undertook.

The General Theory of Capitalist Stagnation

'The real task of an underconsumption theory', Sweezy proposed 'is to demonstrate that capitalism has an inherent *tendency* to expand the capacity to produce consumption goods more rapidly than the demand for consumption goods.' Such a tendency may be manifested in two forms. Where an increase in capacity leads to overproduction and then curtailment of production, 'the tendency in question manifests itself in a crisis'. In a second case, however, capacity is *not* expanded 'because it is realized that the additional capacity would be redundant relative to the demand for the commodities it could produce. In this case, the tendency does not manifest itself in a crisis, but rather in stagnation of production' (p. 180).

As Sweezy noted, in *either* case the existence of such a tendency significantly alters the fundamental questions economists must pose. Marx's comments in *Capital* imply, Sweezy argued (p. 107), that:

> stagnation of production, in the sense of less-than-capacity utilization of productive resources, is to be regarded as the normal state of affairs under capitalist conditions. If this view is adopted, the whole crisis problem appears in a new light. Emphasis shifts from the question: 'What brings on crisis and depression?' to its opposite: 'What brings on expansion?'

Here was the core of Sweezy's argument. It is one to which he has returned in various forms over the years. As he commented in 1980, 'if a monopoly capitalist economy tends towards stagnation — in the same sense that it always used to be assumed that a competitive capitalist economy tends towards full employment — then the problem to be explained is periods of sustained expansion and buoyancy'.[25] Much, indeed, of his work can be seen as a variation around this theme, which was to become a *leitmotiv*.

It is actually more accurate to describe Sweezy's argument in *The Theory of Capitalist Development* as an over-accumulation theory of crisis than as one of underconsumption. In the model presented, crisis is not triggered by an increase in the rate of exploitation (rate of surplus value) or by inadequate effective demand. Rather, it is the result of excessive additions to capacity; a relative expansion of fixed capital occurs (in the Appendix version of his argument) because of an increase in the propensity of capitalists to invest and a tendency to substitute machinery for direct labour.

Assuming a constant relation between additions to means of production and potential additions to output, the expansion of capacity tends to exceed that which would be warranted: the actual increase in the demand for consumption goods is insufficient to justify those previous investment decisions. In this argument (as in early writings of Kalecki), the essential recognition is that investment is not only a component of aggregate demand: it also, importantly, increases productive capacity.

The central problem in the argument, however, is that if the sector producing means of production expands sufficiently, there *will* be adequate income generated in that sector to warrant capacity increases in the consumption goods sector — a point not recognised explicitly in the model. Sweezy's crisis theory then amounted to the argument that this condition would not *normally* be satisfied: thus, the general tendency would be one toward underconsumption/over-accumulation.

To understand why equilibrating growth in Department 1 (the sector producing means of production) was seen as a *special* case, we have to go back to Sweezy's comments on the argument of Tugan-Baranowski. As Sweezy noted, Tugan demonstrated that the balance could easily be achieved if 'social production were organized in accordance with a plan'. In short, 'if the proportional division of output is precisely that which is prescribed by the equilibrium condition for expanded reproduction, then supply and demand must be in exact balance' (p. 166). Yet, such a condition as the *normal* case was contrary to the specific characteristic of capitalism — that it is a system in which the very purpose of production is not the harmonization of production but the expansion of capital.

This did not mean that the prescribed equilibrium condition could not be achieved; it *could* — under special circumstances. (Indeed, in Sweezy's Appendix model, the general tendency would not exist at all if national income were growing at an increasing rate, which he suggested might be characteristic of a 'young' capitalist country.) As Marx had done in presenting his discussion of the tendency of the rate of profit to fall, Sweezy followed his discussion of the general tendency toward underconsumption/ over-accumulation with a consideration of 'counteracting forces'. Precisely because there were such counteracting causes, Sweezy proposed 'that for long periods the latter (tendency to underconsumption) may remain latent and inoperative' (p. 180).

The establishment of new industries was one such important counteracting force. Reminiscent of Schumpeter's business cycle theory, in so far as the period of initial investments did not add correspondingly to output of consumption goods, the tendency was suspended; only when this process was completed and new consumption goods could come on stream was the general relation between additions to means of production and additions to consumption demand re-established. In this case (as well as that of faulty investment and state expenditures), the counteracting tendency exists to the extent that there is an increase in aggregate demand but not a corresponding increase in capacity.

Yet, Sweezy proposed that the strength of new industries as a counteracting force was dependent upon the relative share of total investment absorbed; although new industries would always continue to appear, their relative importance would decline as a country industrialised. 'One of the most powerful forces counteracting the ever-present tendency to underconsumption', was thus disappearing (p. 220). It was not, however, the only such sea change.

A declining rate of population growth meant the dramatic eclipse of yet another of developed capitalism's critical counteracting forces. In stressing the relation between declining population growth and stagnation (a relation epitomised as 'the law of inverse relation between population growth and the tendency to underconsumption'), Sweezy was, of course, by no means alone (p. 224). Alvin Hansen's 1938 Presidential Address to the American Economics Association, 'Economic progress and declining population growth', had put this issue high on the list of explanations of the continuing sluggishness of the 1930s.[26]

Yet, rather than emphasising the beneficial effects upon *demand*, as Hansen had, Sweezy identified rapid population growth as extremely favourable to the expansion of capitalism because it ensured available reserves of labour. With the pressure to substitute machinery for labour therefore reduced, it followed from Sweezy's model that the danger of underconsumption was not present. In the weakening, then, of these counteracting forces, Sweezy found an explanation for the progressive strengthening of the tendency to underconsumption. The prospect for mature and developed capitalist countries, thus, was increasingly one of chronic stagnation (p. 226). 'So far as capitalism is concerned', he commented, 'we are undoubtedly justified in calling underconsumption a disease of old age' (p. 189).

But, what about the role of monopoly? Given Sweezy's earlier work, it appears as a strange failure that the growth of monopoly plays no role in this conclusion. After all, from the rigid prices and absence of price competition under conditions of oligopoly to the 'vast internal financial resources' of the large firms to the significance (noted in his thesis) of large-scale industry and combination in fostering excess capacity and the contraction of investment outlets, there was an explanation both for a growing tendency to underconsumption/over-accumulation and for this to be increasingly manifested in stagnation rather than crisis.

The Theory of Capitalist Development was not silent on the question of monopoly. In a later section, Sweezy described the tendency for higher prices and profits in the concentrated sectors, the disinclination to expand output in these sectors (because of the potential effect upon the profit rate), an increased bias toward labour-saving innovation and the possibility that the growth of monopoly would lead to an increased rate of surplus value thereby strengthening the tendency to underconsumption (pp. 274–277). The effect of monopoly, in this respect, was clearly to *intensify* the inherent tendency of capitalism. On the other hand, Sweezy identified the growth of selling costs as the result of the non-price competition characteristic of concentrated industries as a counteracting force (p. 283); this was the only one of the monopoly-related characteristics considered explicitly in the explanation of the general tendency to stagnation.

Why was the discussion of monopoly not at the *centre* of Sweezy's theory of underconsumption? Because *something else* was there — Keynes and the secular stagnation argument of his foremost North American champion, Alvin Hansen (who joined the Harvard faculty in 1937). For, without question, Sweezy was profoundly influenced by Keynes and Hansen. As he noted in 1946, 'the sense of liberation and the intellectual stimulation that *The General Theory* immediately produced' may only be appreciated fully by those trained as economists in the period before 1936.[27] Similarly, reviewing Hansen's *Full Recovery or Stagnation?* in 1938, he described the latter's analysis as 'brilliant and profound'; and, several years later, he hailed Hansen's contribution to a 'rebirth of scientific economics'.[28] Certainly the influence, in particular, of Hansen can be seen — not only in *The Theory of Capitalist Development* but also in a volume published in 1938 in which Sweezy collaborated, *An Economic Program for American Democracy*.[29]

Was Sweezy at the time, then, simply a left-wing Keynesian? Although there were elements in *The Theory of Capitalist Development* clearly drawing upon Keynes and Hansen, that is not sufficient to yield the conclusion that Sweezy can be considered a Keynesian — any more than Marx can be considered a Ricardian for similar reasons.[30] At issue is the framework within which those elements were incorporated. While Sweezy followed Hansen, for example, in stressing the importance of declining population growth, he offered an entirely different explanation — just as Marx had with the classical theories such as the falling rate of profit. More than anything else, Sweezy's work appears as a *critique* of the Keynesians from a Marxian perspective.

Rather than focusing upon the Keynesian elements in Sweezy, the real question is how Keynes, working within the neoclassical framework, came up with an argument so easily absorbed within a Marxian framework. As Marx had argued that the political economists did not understand the underlying basis of their own laws (theories), so also did Sweezy consistently stress that the Keynesians knew *what* was occurring in the Depression but did not understand *why*. ('Hansen understands very well what is wrong with our present-day economy, and that is all to the good. But ask the question of this book: why have matters turned out as they have? You will not find much by way of answer.'[31]) The adequacy of proposed Keynesian solutions was, of course, the central problem.

The Keynesians, Sweezy indicated, did not see that the troubles were 'manifestations of the real nature of the capitalist system itself'.[32] Thus, while Keynes 'was able to demonstrate that his fellow economists, by their unthinking acceptance of Say's Law, were in effect asserting the impossibility of what was actually happening', Sweezy argued that Keynes was unable to proceed to a critique of existing society. Why? Because Keynes attributed the problems to 'a failure of intelligence and not to the breakdown of a social system'.[33] 'In general', Sweezy commented, 'one can say that to the Keynesians the crisis of capitalism appears as a crisis of intelligence.'[34]

Nevertheless, Sweezy emphasised that, when it came to a clarification of the 'functioning of the capitalist mechanism', Marxists had much 'to learn from the work of Keynes and his followers'.[35] Indeed, some of Marx's work, he argued, 'takes on a new meaning and fits into its proper place when read in the light of the Keynesian contributions'.[36] And, he continues to stress today that Marxists should not be afraid to learn from Keynes since 'most of the valuable Keynesian insights can be added' to the basic structure of Marxism.[37]

Yet it was not many years before Sweezy would identify problems in *The Theory of Capitalist Development* as related to the general Keynesian intellectual environment in which he had been working. Initially, as he indicated in a 1950 response to Evsey Domar and several Japanese critics of his book, Sweezy declared his exposition of underconsumption crises in terms of net aggregates to be 'one of the weakest parts of the book' and argued that his aggregative analysis (attributable to Keynesian influence) was not suitable for exploring the question of underconsumption.[38] In subsequent years, however, he became increasingly critical of the failure of Keynesian theory precisely because it was 'wholly on the macro level'.[39] The missing micro-element was that of monopoly.

The General Theory in the Golden Age[40]

Upon Sweezy's return to Harvard after the war it became clear that there were no prospects of being rehired with tenure after the completion of his existing contract. Although supported by Schumpeter for a tenure-track position, 'there was never any chance that they would take a Marxist'. Accordingly, financially secure enough not to have to rely upon an academic salary, Sweezy resigned his position and proceeded to work with Leo Huberman to establish *Monthly Review*.[41]

In its opening issue in May 1949, Sweezy noted recent government evidence confirming 'a phenomenon of great and growing importance, the extent to which the huge corporate giants now finance their expansion internally... and have consequently become independent of the capital markets generally and of banker control in particular'.[42] He repeated his argument that the normal tendency of American capitalism was one of chronic depression and mass unemployment.

In the context of post-war boom, however, Sweezy now had to explain why things looked different. It was not difficult — the massive military expenditures for World War II and the armaments build up of the post-war period. Depression or stagnation rather than a full employment equilibrium, he argued in a 1952 restatement of his theory, must be regarded as the normal condition of developed capitalism; yet, new industries were a central factor capable of 'taking up the slack'. If these new industries are 'sufficiently numerous and important they may keep the system going at or near full capacity'.[43] In the development of the military–industrial complex, Sweezy had found a new and important counteracting force making the tendency to underconsumption 'latent and inoperative' in the post-war period.[44]

In the course of the Golden Age, however, Sweezy's theory was to undergo a quite significant shift: a new element was to enter. Describing his theory in 1980, he indicated that it 'draws upon or combines a line of thought which originated with Michal Kalecki and attained its most complete expression in the work of Josef Steindl, published in the early 1950s, *Maturity and Stagnation in American Capitalism*'. Despite the 'strange failure of Keynesian theory' to make the connection between monopoly (at the micro-level) and stagnation (at the macro-level), Kalecki *had* integrated the two. 'And of course it was Kalecki's lead that Steindl followed up.'[45]

This acknowledgement of theoretical influence had appeared earlier in the book he had written with Paul Baran, *Monopoly Capital* (which Sweezy described as a 'simpler version' of the Kalecki/Steindl argument). There, Baran and Sweezy praised Kalecki and Steindl for their integration of monopoly at the micro-level into their macro-models. And, they noted, 'anyone familiar with the work of Kalecki and Steindl will readily recognize that the authors of the present work owe a great deal to them'.[46]

Without question, the catalyst was Steindl's book, which Sweezy described in his 1971 Marshall Lecture as 'one of the most important and most neglected works of political economy of the last half century'.[47] That appreciation is recorded as well in his 1954 review of Steindl's book, where Sweezy proposed that, 'in successfully linking up the theory of investment with the theory of imperfect competition he has, I believe, made a contribution of the first importance'.

It is interesting what appeared at the time central to Sweezy. He summarised Steindl's theory as stressing that 'the driving force behind capital accumulation is internal corporate saving'. In a competitive industry, those savings were responsive to demand: with a shortage of productive capacity, the resulting high profit margins would increase internal savings and thus accumulation; similarly, excess productive capacity would generate competition which would drive down profit margins and thus internal savings.

In oligopolistic industries, however, excess capacity was *not* remedied in this way because price competition was avoided and 'for this reason there is a *permanent* bias in favor of high profit margins and excess capacity'. Further, excess capacity discourages additional investment whereas a variety of factors inhibit a flow of investment to competitive sectors. Thus, in Steindl's theory, there was an explanation of a long-term stagnation in capital accumulation linked to a secular decline in competition.[48]

As we have seen, however, *all these elements were already present in Sweezy's own work*! On the other hand, providing an organising principle for those elements could be seen as a central contribution. The place to examine the new combination is in *Monopoly Capital*, upon which Baran and Sweezy began work in the spring of 1956 while Baran was in the process of completing his *Political Economy of Growth*.[49]

As they noted in their introduction, it was a work generated by, among other things, a dissatisfaction with the adequacy of existing Marxist analyses (including their own) of monopoly capitalism. Marxist theory could explain well the Depression of the 1930s, but fell short in dealing with a post-war period in which severe depression had not reoccurred. 'Nor have Marxists contributed significantly', they commented, 'to our understanding of some of the major characteristics of the "affluent society" — particularly its colossal capacity to generate private and public waste and the profound economic, political, and cultural consequences which flow from this feature of the system.'[50]

At the core of the 'stagnation of Marxian social science' was the failure to place monopoly at the very centre of analysis. The project, an attempt to 'remedy this situation in an explicit and indeed radical fashion', was organised around 'one central theme: the generation and absorption of the surplus under conditions of monopoly capitalism'.[51]

Aside from the apparent terminological shift from surplus value to the concept of the 'surplus', what stands out immediately here is the concept of the *absorption* of the surplus. Both aspects had been considered explicitly by Baran in his book (which had drawn upon Kalecki and Steindl as well as upon Sweezy). Indeed, writing to

Sweezy in 1956 upon reading the galleys of *The Political Economy of Growth*, he had expressed the hope that the discussion of monopoly capitalism would help to push 'Marxist thought on Mono. Cap. off its dead center and into a deepened consideration of what we both agree is the crux of the matter: the generation and absorption of the economic surplus'.[52]

As a concept, generation of the surplus did not present any particular difficulties at first sight. The opening discussion explored the ability of the large corporations to maintain high prices (and to avoid price competition) while at the same time cutting production costs. The lion's share of rising productivity thus captured, the projection was one of 'continuously widening profit margins'; unlike Sweezy's earlier argument, at the core was a growing rate of exploitation in the sphere of production.[53]

Implied, then, was a growth in the profit share of national product and, indeed, 'a law of monopoly capitalism that the surplus tends to rise both absolutely and relatively as the system develops' (p. 72). Yet, as Baran and Sweezy stressed in response to an argument by Nicholas Kaldor, this relative growth of the surplus would not necessarily be *apparent* in the national statistical accounts. The issue was one of 'the problem of realizing surplus value', a problem more chronic than in Marx's time. For, only profits which are *realised* are recorded: 'potential profits .. leave their traces in the statistical record in the paradoxical form of unemployment and excess capacity' (p. 76).

The genealogy of this argument is clear. It originated with Kalecki:

> Imagine, for instance, that as a result of the increase in the degree of monopoly the relative share of profits in the gross income rises. Profits will remain unchanged because they continue to be determined by investment which depends on past investment decisions, but the real wages and salaries and the gross income or product will fall. The level of income or product will fall. The level of income or product will decline to the point at which the higher relative share of profits yield the same absolute level of profits.[54]

Although Kalecki had considered the possibility of 'retarded growth' and the potential for growth of unutilised capacity, the immediate influence on *Monopoly Capital* came from Steindl. The reason, he had argued, why we do not observe a decrease in the wage share of income (or an increase in the profit share of income) as the gross profit margin rises is because the rise in the profit share exists only *potentially*; that is, it exists only as a tendency. Thus, the rise of oligopoly increases the production of surplus value, but the latter:

> can be realized only to the extent to which there is a corresponding amount of investment and capitalists' consumption. If this amount does not increase, then the rise in the rate of surplus value *produced* will not lead to any increase in surplus value realized, but only to excess capacity.

For Steindl, then, the effect of a growing rate of exploitation in the sphere of production would not be reflected in an actual increase in the surplus secured but, rather, by a reduced degree of capacity utilisation 'so that there is not a shift of actual income from wages to profits, but a shift of potential income of workers to wastage in excess capacity'.[55] It is the same point that Baran made in the foreword to the 1962 edition of *The Political Economy of Growth*. Responding to Kaldor's criticism, he argued that a rising surplus is entirely compatible with a constant (and even rising) share of wages in national income 'simply because the increment of surplus assumes the form of an increment of *waste*' (p. xxi).

The same point — and yet not quite the same. For, what had occurred was a *generalisation* of the category of 'waste'. As *Monopoly Capital* would indicate subsequently, the rising surplus can be absorbed or utilised in several ways: '(1) it can be consumed, (2) it can be invested, and (3) it can be wasted' (p. 79). Given the normal inability (always present in Sweezy's theory) of capitalist consumption and investment to absorb the surplus that monopoly capitalism was capable of producing, 'waste' (in the form of 'the sales effort', government expenditures and imperialism) now edged its way on to centre stage in the analysis.

Thus, what prevented the growth of excess capacity (one form of waste) which the Kalecki/Steindl theory would predict as the rate of exploitation rose was the growing reliance upon *other* forms of waste. Growing relative to capitalist consumption and investment, 'they increasingly dominate the composition of social output, the rate of economic growth, and the quality of society itself' (p. 114). These were the days, remember, not of the Depression but of Galbraith's *Affluent Society*, Vance Packard's *The Waste Makers* and the Edsel.[56] What was to be explained, in the context of a general theory of capitalist stagnation, was the relation between the 'colossal capacity to generate private and public waste' and the absence of depression. Here, the treatment of the Sales Effort was representative.

Although Marx had treated the expenses associated with selling commodities as a deduction from the total surplus value, Baran and Sweezy proposed that the sales effort had 'come to play a role, both quantitatively and qualitatively, beyond anything Marx ever dreamed of' (p. 114). And, essentially, that new role was that advertising and other selling expenditures had become an important 'mode of utilization of the economic surplus' (p. 125). It was a waste of resources, 'but in the presence of unemployment and idle capacity, these resources would have otherwise remained unutilized: advertising calls into being a net addition to investment and income' (p. 127).

This was a shift in position. Sweezy had earlier argued that growing sales expenses act as a counteracting force to the general tendency of capitalism toward underconsumption/over-accumulation in so far as they diverted expanding productive forces 'into socially unnecessary and hence wasteful channels'.[57] In *Monopoly Capital*, however, this waste of resources not only increased output but also 'the sales effort absorbs, directly and indirectly, a large amount of surplus which otherwise would not have been produced' (p. 142).

Clearly, more than the emphasis on the absorption of the surplus was new here. There also was a quite different operative concept— a surplus which would not be produced in the absence of waste such as advertising (but also government expenditures and imperialism). While that concept was consistent with the Kalecki/Steindl framework, here *Monopoly Capital* drew some of its distinctive characteristics from Baran. What had occurred was a shift from the concept of 'actual surplus' to that of 'potential surplus', i.e. to the surplus which would be both produced and realised at the full employment level. As Baran had noted, the concept differed explicitly from Marx's surplus value by including 'the output lost in view of underemployment or misemployment of productive resources'.[58]

In the context of Baran's own work on underdeveloped countries, the emphasis on the 'utilization of available or underutilized resources' and the need to mobilise the potential economic surplus for the development of productive forces echoed the concerns of classical economists (and his own early teacher, Evgenii Preobrazhensky).[59] Extension of the concept of potential surplus to monopoly capitalism, though, involved an important shift of focus. As Harry Magdoff had noted in relation to Baran's development of the concept, the potential surplus 'is an active, operative concept: it leads to an understanding of the waste, inefficiency, and unfulfilled possibilities of monopoly capitalism'.[60]

The system, for Baran, required waste to absorb 'the overflowing economic surplus' or to provide 'an adequate stimulus to additional investment by expanding aggregate demand'; and in this respect *Monopoly Capital* followed his argument.[61] Not simply drawing upon Kalecki and Steindl for the connection between monopoly and the tendency to stagnation, the book also extended Kalecki's treatment of a budget deficit and export surplus to the category of waste in incorporating the concept of the potential economic surplus.[62] The latter, however, was not an unproblematic element — especially with respect to the attempt to determine the potential surplus by adding to profits (and other property income) the various components of waste.[63] Yet, in combination with the Kalecki/Steindl framework, it enabled *Monopoly Capital* to offer an answer to its two questions: why a severe depression had not reoccurred and why monopoly capitalism was a waste land.

For those who had not lived through the experience of the Depression, it was the *second* question (rather than the first) which was central. In the 1930s, Sweezy had asked the timely question why capitalism had a tendency to chronic unemployment and stagnation. In capitalism's Golden Age, *Monopoly Capital* now asked a question equally as timely. Its answers found a receptive audience in the generation emerging from the desert of the Cold War, whose only experience had been that of the post-war boom.

There was another important question, though. As Baran and Sweezy noted, there is in *Monopoly Capital* 'almost total neglect of a subject which occupies a central place in Marx's study of capitalism: the labor process'. Questions such as the nature of work, the psychology of workers, the forms of working-class organisation, etc. — 'all obviously important subjects', they acknowledged, 'which would have to be dealt with in any comprehensive study of monopoly capitalism' — were missing.[64] Although Sweezy subsequently proposed that the gap was present because he and Baran lacked 'the necessary qualifications' — the 'crucially important direct experience' of the capitalist labour process, the basis for the silence goes somewhat deeper.[65]

In ignoring the labour process, Baran and Sweezy insisted that they had not forgotten class struggle: 'The revolutionary initiative against capitalism, which in Marx's day belonged to the proletariat in the advanced countries, has passed into the hands of the impoverished masses in the underdeveloped countries who are struggling to free themselves from imperialist domination and exploitation'.[66] There was a reason for this. Several years earlier, Sweezy and Huberman had argued that rising wages of steel workers came at the expense of steel consumers and that this was not unique to the particular industry: 'sharing increased monopoly profits between big corporations and strong unions has not been confined to steel but rather has been quite general in the monopolistically organized sectors of the economy'.

The capitalist labour process, and workers, thus disappeared as subjects in *Monopoly Capital* because workers in monopoly capitalism were not themselves seen to be acting as subjects.[67] Organised labour had consigned itself 'to playing the role of junior partner in a Big Business-dominated society'.[68] In a country lacking not only a revolutionary movement but also a Labour Party, such a judgement was not surprising.[69] Sweezy expanded upon this point in 1967 noting that production workers had been able to capture a portion of the substantial increases in productivity but also citing Lenin's argument that imperialist 'booty' permits capitalists to 'bribe and win over to their side an aristocracy of labor'.[70]

Monopoly Capital thus answered another question: what happened to the working class? A less rather than more revolutionary proletariat in the developed countries was an inherent characteristic of the era of monopoly capital. Yet, capitalism had to be understood as a 'global system embracing both the (relatively few) industrializing countries and their (relatively numerous) satellites and dependencies'; and, in that global system, the revolutionary subjects had become 'the masses in these exploited dependencies'.[71] It had become increasingly clear in the post-war period, Sweezy concluded in 1971, that 'the principal contradiction in the system, at least in the present historical period, is not *within* the developed part but *between* the developed and underdeveloped parts'.[72] That answer, too, found a receptive audience in a generation struggling against US imperial involvement in Vietnam and elsewhere around the world.

The General Theory in a New Age of Crisis

In the retardation in economic growth which became apparent in the early 1970s, Sweezy has found confirmation that, sooner or later, the inherent tendency of monopoly capitalism toward stagnation exerts itself. The period of the 1970s and 1980s has thus been an opportunity to restate his theory in a context in which the effect of the tendency rather than that of the counteracting forces is manifest. Since this period has also been one marked by his collaboration with Harry Magdoff (who before the onset of McCarthyism had, among other things, served as the head of the current business analysis section of the US Department of Commerce), it has meant that there has been a strong empirical element in Sweezy's work in this period.[73]

More than a restatement of the theory, however, has occurred. Significantly, in his explanations as to why the tendency to stagnation was latent and inoperative for so long a period, the centrality of waste as a category has faded from the analysis — as has any consideration of the concept of potential surplus. Waste, despite its thematic prominence, had never been the *sole* 'counteracting force' identified in *Monopoly Capital*: new industries and wars (and their aftermath) had remained part of the analysis. Thus, a wave of 'automobilization' in the context of post-war consumer liquidity as well as the enormous increase in arms spending were identified by Baran and Sweezy as important explanations of the post-war boom.[74] Similarly, Sweezy and Huberman emphasised in *Monthly Review* the importance of the post-war reconstruction boom of Western Europe and the stimulus of growing trade within the Common Market; within a year of the publication of *Monopoly Capital* their list of factors explaining the boom included military spending, deficit finance, tax subsidies and the growth of consumer debt (but not 'waste' as such).[75]

To this list has been added the civilian spin-off from military technology and, especially, US post-war economic hegemony (with its particular implications for the growth of world trade and capital). The specific combination of these factors, Sweezy argues, was sufficient to produce a unique stimulus to investment; it meant a major investment boom in key industries and rapid growth of capacity in all the leading capitalist economies (as well as some Third World countries).

The war, indeed, 'altered the givens of the world economic situation'; a unique set of events had provided powerful counteracting forces. Yet, 'every one of the forces which powered the long post-war expansion was, and was bound to be, self-limiting'.[76] And so, with the exhaustion of the special conditions, there followed increased levels of unemployment, excess capacity (on a world scale) and lagging investment — stagnation both realised and operative.[77]

The displacement of waste was not the only change to Sweezy's general theory of stagnation in the 1970s and 1980s. *Monopoly Capital* had focused upon characteristics reflecting the unique post-war position of US corporations relatively secure from capitalist competitors of other countries; and, as US international economic hegemony declined, so too did monopoly slip from the centre of the analysis.

In Sweezy's *Four Lectures on Marxism* (1981), the focus was upon the inherent tendency of capitalism toward over-accumulation, the tendency for productive power to grow 'more rapidly than is warranted by society's consuming power'. In this context, the significance attributed to monopoly was that it 'intensified' the contradictions of the accumulation process — both by enhancing the ability to accumulate and by choking off outlets for investment. More stress, similarly, was placed upon the significance of 'maturity' in the explanation as to why counteracting forces (such as, in particular, the effect of new industries) tend to become weaker.[78] *In a very real sense, Sweezy returned in this period to earlier formulations of his theory.*

The Kalecki/Steindl link between monopoly at the micro-level and stagnation at the macro-level, however, has remained integral to his argument: 'the more monopolistic the economy, the stronger the tendency to stagnation'.[79] Stagnation, Sweezy argues, is a 'consequence of the specific form of overaccumulation of capital which characterizes capitalism in its monopoly phase'. Any attempt at analysis of developed capitalism, accordingly, must recognise the importance of monopolistic elements. Precisely because of its failure to incorporate this micro-element, Sweezy has argued that

Keynesian theory could not explain the emergence of 'stagnation' in the 1970s.[80]

In the course of interpreting and analysing current developments from the perspective of his general theory, Sweezy (in conjunction with Magdoff) has made *Monthly Review* during this period a unique medium in which to trace the changing fortunes of US capitalism. Two such developments have been of particular interest. In the 'embryo of an adequate theory of inflation under conditions of monopoly capitalism', Sweezy and Magdoff argued in 1974 that the power of giant corporations to control prices and wages intensified the tendency toward stagnation; at the same time, however, it meant that attempts to stimulate the economy generated inflation.[81] Having ignored 'the monopolistic structure of the economy', however, (bastard) Keynesian technicians accordingly were confounded in their efforts to stimulate a stagnating economy because 'much of the increase in monetary demand was dissipated in inflationary price increases rather than in expanded output'.[82]

In addition to stagflation, the theoretical issue which Sweezy has explored most in recent years is the growth of financial speculation. After years of noting the growth of debt (both private and public), he has increasingly called attention to the coexistence of a stagnant production sector and a prosperous and expanding financial sector. In 1983 Sweezy and Magdoff emphasised that a growing part of money capital was not directly transformed into productive capital but was used instead to purchase financial instruments. There was no necessity, however, for this money to find its way, directly or indirectly, into real capital formation. 'It may just as well remain in the form of money capital circulating around in the financial sector, fueling the growth of financial markets which increasingly take on a life of their own.'[83]

Following two years in which financial transactions proliferated and new financial instruments (options on futures, etc.) multiplied, Magdoff and Sweezy suggested that 'the financial sphere has the potential to become an autonomous subsystem of the economy as a whole, with an enormous capacity for self-expansion'. In that growing divergence between a stagnant economy and a financial explosion, however, they noted in 1985 that one definite possibility was 'a bust of classic dimensions'. Indeed, the most remarkable thing was that it had not yet occurred.[84]

But why has this been happening? Sweezy and Magdoff have recently argued that behind the financial explosion has been a growing concentration of wealth and income. There has been:

> a swelling of the pool of fresh savings seeking profitable investment outlets. However, since the demands on this pool for investment in the production of real goods and services have been declining, more and more of it has been flowing into purely financial channels, giving rise to a vast expansion of the financial superstructure of the economy and an unparalleled explosion of speculative activity of all kinds.[85]

The explanation is entirely consistent with Sweezy's general theory of stagnation. (It can also be related to the discussions by Kalecki and Steindl of 'rentiers' and 'outside' savings, respectively.)[86] In this respect, it may confirm Sweezy's often-repeated view that understanding stagnation as the 'normal' state of a developed capitalist economy is a far more fruitful assumption than the full-employment assumption which underlies neoclassical economics.

Whether it is sufficient for Sweezy, on the other hand, is another matter; he has become increasingly dissatisfied with the adequacy of our understanding of the relation between the spheres of finance and production: 'In economics, we need a theory which integrates finance and production, the circuits of capital of a financial and a real productive character much more effectively than our traditional theories do'.[87]

Paul Sweezy continues to analyse the characteristics of a mature capitalist economy — work begun more than half a century ago. The Dean of radical economics remains an eager student of history, tracing the new forms of the stagnationist tendencies of monopoly capitalism. In all this, he retains the enthusiasm of his youth. Even his earlier pessimism about workers in developed capitalist economies has been tempered with the passage of the Golden Age: if 'the global system has now entered a crisis phase that gives every sign of being irreversible, it is hard to avoid the conclusion that we are entering a new chapter in the history of the metropolitan working classes'.[88]

No one would be happier than Paul Sweezy himself. He ended, indeed, his foreword to Harry Braverman's *Labour and Monopoly Capital*: 'The sad, horrible heart-breaking way the vast majority of my fellow countrymen and women, as well as their counterparts in most of the rest of the world, are obliged to spend their working lives is seared into my consciousness in an excruciating and unforgettable manner'.[89]

To help put an end to such a situation remains the goal of Paul Sweezy at the age of 79. That, indeed, is the lesson that he draws from his general theory of stagnation: it 'teaches us that what we need is not the reform of monopoly capitalism but its replacement by a system that organizes economic activity not for the greater glory of capital but to meet the needs of people to live decent, secure, and to the extent possible, creative lives'.[90]

Notes

1. Lawrence S. Lifshultz, 'Could Karl Marx teach economics in America?', *Ramparts*, vol. 12, no. 9, 1974, p. 54.
2. Meghnad Desai, *Marxian Economics*, Basil Blackwell, 1979, pp. 1-2.
3. Gerd Hardach, Dieter Karras and Ben Fine, *A Short History of Socialist Economic Thought*, Edward Arnold, 1978, p. 60.
4. Paul M. Sweezy, 'Toward a critique of economics', *Monthly Review*, January, 1970, reprinted in Paul M. Sweezy, *Modern Capitalism and Other Essays*, Monthly Review Press, 1972, p. 58.
5. 'Interview with Paul M. Sweezy', *Monthly Review*, April 1987, p. 15.
6. Michael Hillard, 'Harry Magdoff and Paul Sweezy: biographical notes', in Stephen Resnick and Richard Wolff (eds), *Rethinking Marxism: Essays for Harry Magdoff & Paul Sweezy*, Autonomedia, New York, 1985, p. 400.
7. Lifshultz, 'Could Karl Marx teach economics', p. 55; 'Interview with Paul Sweezy', p. 8.
8. Hillard, 'Harry Magdoff and Paul Sweezy'; Paul M. Sweezy, *Four Lectures on Marxism*, Monthly Review Press, 1981, pp. 12–13.
9. Paul M. Sweezy, 'Preface', *The Theory of Capitalist Development: Principles of Marxian Political Economy*, Monthly Review Press, 1956, p. vi.
10. Paul M. Sweezy, 'Introduction' to Joseph A. Schumpeter, *Imperialism and Social Classes*, Augustus M. Kelley, New York, 1951, pp. xxii–xxv.
11. 'Interview with Paul Sweezy', p. 5.
12. *Ibid.*
13. *Ibid.*, p. 2; Hillard, 'Harry Magdoff and Paul Sweezy', p. 401.
14. 'Interest groups in the American economy', in National Resources Committee, *The Structure of the American Economy*, Part 1, Appendix 13, 1939, reprinted in Paul M. Sweezy, *The Present as History: Essays and Reviews on Capitalism and Socialism*, Monthly Review Press, 1953.
15. Paul M. Sweezy, 'The decline of the investment banker', *Antioch*

Review, Spring 1941, reprinted in *The Present as History*, pp. 192, 195.
16. Paul M. Sweezy, *The Theory of Capitalist Development*, pp. 166–169.
17. Paul M. Sweezy, *Monopoly and Competition in the English Coal Trade, 1550-1850*, Harvard University Press, 1938, p. 119.
18. *Ibid.*, pp. 148–149.
19. Paul M. Sweezy, 'Demand under conditions of oligopoly', *Journal of Political Economy*, 1939, reprinted in American Economics Association, *Readings in Price Theory*, Richard D. Irwin, 1952.
20. *Ibid.*, p. 406. Information on the 1938 American Economics Association meetings comes from the *Proceedings* and Paul M. Sweezy.
21. Michel De Vroey, 'Value, production and exchange', in Ian Steedman *et al. The Value Controversy*, Verso, 1981, p. 173; see also Diane Elson, 'The value theory of labour', in Diane Elson (ed.), *Value: The Representation of Labour in Capitalism*, CSE Books, 1979, pp. 116–122 ff.
22. See, for example, Bruce McFarlane, *Radical Economics*, St. Martins Press, 1982, p. 139.
23. *Journal of Economic Literature*, June 1974, pp.482–483.
24. Shigeto Tsuru, 'Mr Dobb and Marx's theory of value', reprinted in Shigeto Tsuru, *Towards A New Political Economy (Collected Works of Shigeto Tsuru)*, vol. 13, Kodansha, Tokyo, 1976, p. 99.
25. 'The crisis of American capitalism', *Monthly Review*, October 1980, p. 3.
26. Alvin Hansen, *American Economic Review*, March, 1939, reprinted in American Economics Association, *Readings in Business Cycle Theory*, Richard D. Irwin, 1951.
27. Paul M. Sweezy, 'John Maynard Keynes', *Science and Society*, Fall, 1946, reprinted in *The Present as History*, p. 257, note.
28. Alvin Hansen, *Full Recovery or Stagnation?*, W.W. Norton, 1938; 'Hansen and the crisis of capitalism', reprinted in *The Present as History*, pp. 268–270.
29. Richard Gilbert *et al.*, *An Economic Program for American Democracy*, Vanguard, 1938. See the discussion in Robert Lekachman, *The Age of Keynes*, Random House, 1966, pp. 154–156
30. Sweezy has himself suggested this analogy in 'Keynes as a critic of capitalism', *Monthly Review*, April 1981, p. 34.
31. *The Present as History*, p. 272.
32. *Ibid.*, p. 273.
33. 'John Maynard Keynes', p. 258.
34. 'Marxian and orthodox economics', *Science and Society*, Summer 1947, reprinted in *The Present as History*, p. 313.
35. *The Present as History*, p. 315.
36. 'John Maynard Keynes', *ibid.*, p. 261.
37. 'Interview with Paul M. Sweezy', p. 18.
38. 'A reply to critics', *The Economic Review* April 1950, reprinted in *The Present as History*, pp. 353–354, 360.
39. Sweezy, 'The crisis of American capitalism', p. 3.

40. An excellent collection of essays by (among others) Sweezy, Kalecki and Steindl relevant to the discussion in this section may be found in John Bellamy Foster and Henryk Szlajfer (eds), *The Faltering Economy: The Problem of Accumulation under Monopoly Capitalism*, Monthly Review Press, 1984.
41. 'Interview with Paul Sweezy', p. 4; Hillard, 'Harry Magdoff and Paul Sweezy', p. 402.
42. 'Recent developments in American capitalism', *Monthly Review*, May 1949, reprinted in *The Present as History*, p. 118.
43. 'A crucial difference between capitalism and socialism', *The Present as History*, p. 347.
44. See also 'Peace and prosperity', *The Present as History*, p. 364.
45. Sweezy, 'The crisis of American capitalism', pp. 2–3.
46. Paul A. Baran and Paul M. Sweezy, *Monopoly Capital: An Essay on the American Economic and Social Order*, Monthly Review Press, 1966, p. 56.
47. 'On the theory of monopoly capitalism', in Paul M. Sweezy, *Modern Capitalism and Other Essays*, Monthly Review Press, 1972, p. 41.
48. *Econometrica*, October 1954, pp. 531–533.
49. Paul M. Sweezy, 'Paul Alexander Baran: a personal memoir', Paul M. Sweezy and Leo Huberman (eds), *Paul A. Baran (1910–1964): A Collective Portrait*, Monthly Review Press, 1965, p. 29; Paul A. Baran, *The Political Economy of Growth*, Monthly Review Press, 1957.
50. *Monopoly Capital*, p. 3.
51. *Ibid*,. pp. 3–8.
52. 'Paul Alexander Baran: a personal memoir', p. 53.
53. *Monopoly Capital*, p.71.
54. Michel Kalecki, *Theory of Economic Dynamics*, Monthly Review Press, 1968, p. 61.
55. Josef Steindl, *Maturity and Stagnation in American Capitalism*, Monthly Review Press, 1976, p. 245.
56. J. K. Galbraith, *The Affluent Society*, Houghton Mifflin, 1958; Vance Packard, *The Waste Makers*, New York, 1960. The Edsel was a grotesquely styled Ford Car which became an immediate laughing stock on its production.
57. *The Theory of Capitalist Development*, p. 286. See also the discussion in Steindl, *Maturity*, pp. 55–66.
58. *The Political Economy of Growth*, p. 23, note.
59. Paul A. Baran, 'The political economy of backwardness', *Manchester School*, January 1952, reprinted in A.N. Agarwala and S.P. Singh, *The Economics of Underdevelopment*, Oxford University Press, 1958, pp. 81, 83; Isaac Deutscher in *Paul A. Baran: A Collective Portrait*, p. 94.
60. Harry Magdoff, 'The achievement of Paul Baran', in *Paul A. Baran*, p. 77.
61. *The Political Economy of Growth*, pp. 88–92.
62. Kalecki, *Theory of Economic Dynamics*, p. 51.

63. *See, for example, Michael A. Lebowitz, 'Monopoly capital', Studies on the Left*, September-October, 1966. Within this framework, selling expenses and taxes — *to the extent to which they are a charge against surplus value* — reduce the realisable rate of exploitation and thus the slope of the profit share line (i.e. increase output but not profits). It is logical to add these in order to reconstruct the surplus generated within production. Estimating the surplus, however, by adding undifferentiated government expenditures and advertising (according to the theory that these 'absorb' a portion of the surplus) to profits means that profits made possible by the former are counted twice. Cf. Joseph D. Phillips, 'Appendix: estimating the economic surplus', *Monopoly Capital*, pp. 369–391. For a more sympathetic view of the concept of the surplus, see the comprehensive discussion in John Bellamy Foster, *The Theory of Monopoly Capitalism: An Elaboration of Marxian Political Economy* Monthly Review Press, 1968, Chapter 2. See also the essays by Henryk Szlajfer in Foster and Szlajfer, *The Faltering Economy*.
64. *Monopoly Capital*, pp. 8–9.
65. Harry Braverman, *Labor and Monopoly Capital: The Degradation of Work in the Twentieth Century*, Monthly Review Press, 1974, p. x.
66. *Monopoly Capital*, p. 9.
67. The same silence was present in *The Theory of Capitalist Development*. Sweezy's principal concern at that time, though, was to show that mature capitalism had an inherent tendency to stagnation; its failure to provide jobs, in short, was systemic rather than accidental or the result of a failure of intelligence. Those *without* jobs were thus the issue.
68. Leo Huberman and Paul M. Sweezy, 'The steel strike in perspective', *Monthly Review*, February 1960, pp. 357–361.
69. Sweezy and Magdoff subsequently suggested that the theoretical silence in *Monopoly Capital* was in part the reflection of this political silence: 'Marxism leads us to expect an intimate relation between revolutionary theory and revolutionary practise: where either is missing the other will be at the very least severely handicapped'. 'Twenty-five eventful years', *Monthly Review*, June 1974, pp. 7–8.
70. Paul M. Sweezy, 'Marx and the proletariat', *Monthly Review*, December 1967, reprinted in Paul M. Sweezy, *Modern Capitalism and Other Essays*, p. 163.
71. *Ibid.*, pp. 163, 165.
72. Paul M. Sweezy, 'Modern capitalism', *Monthly Review*, June 1971, reprinted in *Modern Capitalism and Other Essays*, p. 13.
73. Hillard, 'Harry Magdoff and Paul Sweezy', p. 397.
74. *Monopoly Capital*, pp. 244–245 and Chapter 8, 'On the history of monopoly capitalism' in general.
75. 'The Common Market', *Monthly Review*, January 1962, p. 391; 'End of the boom?', *Monthly Review*, April 1967, p. 4.
76. 'Why stagnation?', *Monthly Review*, June 1982, reprinted in Harry

Magdoff and Paul Sweezy, *Stagnation and the Financial Explosion*, Monthly Review Press, 1987, pp. 35–36.
77. For a discussion of world excess capacity in the steel industry as 'a harbinger of events to come', see Paul M. Sweezy and Harry Magdoff, 'Steel and stagnation', *Monthly Review*, November 1977.
78. Sweezy, *Four Lectures on Marxism*, pp. 39, 42–43.
79. Sweezy, 'The crisis of American capitalism', p. 3.
80. Paul M. Sweezy, 'The economic crisis in the United States', *Monthly Review*, December 1981, pp. 4, 8.
81. 'Keynesian chickens come home to roost', *Monthly Review*, April 1974, reprinted in Harry Magdoff and Paul M. Sweezy, *The End of Prosperity: The American Economy in the 1970s*, Monthly Review Press, 1977, pp. 21–22.
82. Sweezy, 'The crisis of American capitalism', p. 6; see also 'Inflation without end?', *Monthly Review*, November 1979, p. 9.
83. Harry Magdoff and Paul Sweezy, 'Production and finance', *Monthly Review*, May 1983, reprinted in *Stagnation*, pp. 96–97.
84. 'The financial explosion', *Monthly Review*, December 1985, reprinted in *Stagnation*, pp. 147, 149–150.
85. Harry Magdoff and Paul Sweezy, 'Capitalism and the distribution of income and wealth', *Monthly Review*, October 1987, pp. 13–14.
86. Cf. Kalecki, *Theory of Dynamics*, p. 159; Steindl, *Maturity*, pp. 113–121.
87. 'Interview with Paul Sweezy', p. 19.
88. *Four Lectures on Marxism*, p. 86 note.
89. Braverman, *Labor and Monopoly Capital*, p. xii.
90. 'Introduction', Magdoff and Sweezy, *Stagnation*, p. 25.

Index